GREAT GAMES!

175 GAMES & ACTIVITIES FOR FAMILIES, GROUPS & CHILDREN

·····································

MATTHEW TOONE

TULSA

Library of Congress Catalog-in-Publication Data
ISBN 978-0-9798345-5-4
LOC #2009929284

Müllerhaus Publishing Arts, Inc.
5200 S. Yale Ave. Suite 501
Tulsa, OK 74135

10 9 8 7 6 5 4 3 2 1

Printed in Canada.

TO:

My wonderful wife Heather,
and my incredible sons, Brenden & Nathan
and families everywhere!

INTRODUCTION

IT WAS JUST AFTER MIDNIGHT AND MY FAMILY, A FEW COUSINS, AND
some friends started yet another game of Mafia. You would think that after
having already played three rounds—in addition to spending the early evening
hours playing other fun games—that we all would be a little gamed-out. The
ridiculously large amount of candy, chocolate and popcorn we'd each consumed
was certainly not helping the fact that logic was telling us to stop and go to
bed (plus our stomachs and cheeks were sore from laughing so much). As if
that wasn't enough incentive to stop, those of us with small children knew that
despite the fact that we were having such an incredibly good time, in a few short
hours our babies would inevitably be ready to begin the new day.

It was at this point, and I'll never forget it, that I looked around the room
and quietly observed the people I love so much. I watched my friends and
cousins as they laughed, interacted and smiled, and I began to think about what
had just taken place. More than just playing games, having a blast, laughing and
eating an inappropriately excessive amount of sugar—my wonderful family and
my closest friends were spending time together, creating memories and enjoying
some fun and wholesome entertainment.

Thankfully, while growing up I had many similar settings and experiences in my home. Whether with family, siblings, friends or neighbors, we spent a lot of time together and created some wonderful memories—and much of that time was simply playing games. As my family and friends can attest, I developed a great love and gift for creating new games, thinking of different or better variations of the most common and classic games, and simply collecting any fun game I could.

This book is a dream fulfilled—the result of many years of collecting, creating, compiling and playing the *greatest* family, group and children's games. It is filled with literally hundreds of games for all people everywhere—families, adults, teens and children; groups of all sizes; and it includes games for every possible category and setting!

My hope, however, is that this book will be much more than simply a resource and collection of the greatest games. I hope that these games will bring families together, strengthen relationships, build friendships, create meaningful memories and provide fun, no-cost, uplifting and wholesome entertainment for everyone!

ACKNOWLEDGMENTS

EVERYTHING GOOD IN OUR LIVES SEEMS TO BE THE RESULT OF SOMEONE
else's influence, encouragement or support. It is impossible to acknowledge
everyone who has helped bring this book into print, but I first must thank my
incredible parents for who they are, for their influence and example, and for the
home and environment where they nurtured me. My siblings, who are also my
best friends, have encouraged me to write and compile this book for years—I not
only thank them for that, but for the wonderful memories we share of growing
up playing games and spending TIME together.

The talented people at Müllerhaus are extraordinary. In particular, I must
thank Jodie Nida for her gifted editorial eyes, as well as Douglas Miller for his
exceptional design abilities. And to Gary Locke, my incredible illustrator, whose
work and talents are unrivaled.

Last, and certainly most important, I am grateful to my beautiful wife.
Her encouragement and support not only made this book a reality, she proved
to me that dreams are possible if we only believe we can achieve them, have
faith and take action. We should never quit until our dreams are realized—
and once achieved, we should always seek to bless and help others!

FOREWARD

MY MAIN GOAL IS TO SHOW HOW ANYONE CAN HAVE FUN SIMPLY
playing games! No fancy electronics or expensive gadgets are necessary—just hearts and minds ready for imaginative, interactive play! Please note that every game in this book can be improvised, adapted and changed based on the age group playing, the size of the group, the setting and circumstance, and the competitive nature of those playing.

Many of the children's games can be played and enjoyed by adults, and vice versa. Most outside games can be modified for inside play, while virtually all inside games can be played outside. Road trip games can be changed and played around the living room with the family, while youth group and team-building games can be adjusted to work for smaller groups and families, etc. If a particular game requires six or more people to play, for example, and you only have four people, improvise and adapt accordingly. To ensure the instructions and tips are as easy to understand as possible, I have alternated genders in many of the descriptions. By including the names of fictional players, I hope to illustrate the fun and versatility every game in this book has to offer!

Some games also may require certain things to play—if you do not have those things, simply find a creative alternative. Often a timer is listed—keep in mind that a timer can be anything from a watch with a second hand to a timer from a board game.

Finally, it is important to note that the vast majority of games within this book are competitive in nature. The games' rules and explanations require scoring points to determine a winner. However, each game can also be improvised so that the participants play just to have FUN!

This book is a collection of great family, group and children's games. I created many of these games, others are adaptations of classic games, while some are common games that are extremely popular and played by all. I have created and become acquainted with these games through various situations and life experiences over the years, thus it is impossible to document fully the origin of every game. However, I welcome any information regarding the original source of any game described herein. Once verified, I will give proper credit in future printings of this book.

TABLE OF CONTENTS

CHILDREN'S GAMES

INDOORS

OUTDOORS

MEET THE PLAYERS

ADAM, RACHEL AND THEIR CHILDREN LOVE TO PLAY GAMES! They
are excited to be hosting several game parties for their family, friends and
neighbors. Since most of the adults and children invited to the parties aren't
familiar with the same games, they used this book to explain how many people
it takes to play each game, what supplies are needed, the rules and lots of
fun tips and variations.

To make the rules and details of play easy to follow, we've incorporated the
adventures of Adam, Rachel and all their family, friends and acquaintances into
the descriptions of the games. Join them as they share wonderful times and
discover how easy it is to have fun and find a perfect game for every gathering!

FAMILY & GROUP GAMES
·········· INDOORS ··········

ACT THE ADVERB

 # OF PLAYERS: 3 or more
PLAYERS: Adam, Rachel, John
OBJECTS NEEDED: Nothing

OR MORE

To begin, one person is chosen to leave the room. Adam volunteers to be "it" and leaves while the other players collectively decide on an adverb. For example, they discuss using *humorously, obnoxiously, quietly, forcefully,* etc. (some adjectives work equally well). Adam returns and randomly chooses people to act certain verbs. Each player he chooses must act the verb in the manner of the group's secret adverb. For example, if he chooses Rachel, she'll be acting the group's secret adverb—*quietly*. He may ask her to: walk, eat, dance, sing, read, jump, etc. If he chooses the verb *walk*, Rachel must act like she is *walking*, but do so to convey the idea that she's doing it *quietly*. No talking is allowed while players are acting!

Adam's goal is to guess the group's secret adverb. After Rachel acts *walking*, he guesses what he thinks the adverb is that Rachel portrayed. If he does not correctly guess *quietly*, Adam must ask another person from the group to act the adverb, but he chooses a different verb. This time, he asks Jennifer to *eat*. She begins acting like she's *eating*, but in a way that implies she's doing it *quietly*. If Adam does not guess correctly after the second acting, he gets one more chance. If after the third person acts a verb in the manner of the adverb, and Adam still cannot guess what the adverb is, he does not receive a point. If, however, Adam does guess what the adverb is within three guesses, he gets a point.

The group must choose a new secret adverb each round. Each player takes a turn being "it" and has a chance to win points by guessing. The first person to score five points is the winner!

ALLITERATION

OR MORE

 # OF PLAYERS: 4 or more

PLAYERS: Adam, Rachel, Hannah, Steven

OBJECTS NEEDED: Paper, Pencil, Bowl, Timer

This game may sound easy...but it's not! In preparation, Adam and Rachel have written every letter of the alphabet on small pieces of paper and placed them in a bowl. When their friends arrived, they divided the players into two equal teams. Adam and Rachel are on different teams. To begin, one person from each team goes to the front of the room. Adam and Rachel volunteer to go first. They each draw a letter from the bowl (which ensures they have different letters). When Hannah starts the timer and says, "Go," Adam and Rachel have 30 seconds to say as many real words as possible that start with that letter—but they each must say their words to the *opposing* team.

Each team keeps a tally of how many accurate words are said within 30 seconds. At the end of 30 seconds, Hannah says, "Stop!" and the teams count how many words the opposing teammate said. Teams receive one point for however many *more* words their teammate said. If, for example, Rachel said 24 correct words and Adam only said 18 words—then Rachel's team earns six points (24 - 18 = 6). To start another round, each team sends a new player forward (thus, everyone takes a turn). The first team to reach 100 points is the winner!

VARIATION: To make the game a little more challenging, each round everyone chooses a different category. Sample categories include things like famous people, countries, athletes, subjects in school, animals, cities, etc. After choosing a letter, players must say words within that category that start with the specified letter.

VARIATION: Each round, the group chooses a random qualification of what words can be said. For example, in addition to starting with the chosen letter, the words must also: end with the letter s, have double letters in them, have only one vowel, etc. Another option is to choose two letters out of the bowl and people have to say words that have *both* letters in them. In this variation, allow 1 minute rather than 30 seconds.

BIDDING WAR

OR MORE

 # OF PLAYERS: 4 or more

PLAYERS: Steven, Kyle, Megan, Rachel

OBJECTS NEEDED: Deck of Cards, Paper, Pencil

....

Steven begins the game by dealing eight cards to each player. He places the remaining cards to the side and turns over the top card to determine what *trump* is for that round. For example, if the card turned over is the 6♠, then ♠ is *trump* that round. For ease of bidding and playing, Rachel, Megan, Kyle and Steven organize their cards by suit and in descending order.

To determine what to bid, players look at their hands, then guess how many hands they think they can win based on how many *trump* cards and high cards they are holding. After everyone has looked at their cards and determined how many hands they think they can win, on the count of three, everyone simultaneously holds up the number of fingers that represent how many hands they think they will win that round. Kyle is confident since he's holding several high cards, so he bids four. Megan doesn't think she'll win any hands so she bids zero. Megan knows she'll have to *sluff* (get rid of) all of her cards to keep from winning any hands and make her bid. After the other players bid, Rachel jots down each bid and the game begins!

A hand is won by playing the highest card in the same suit that was led, or playing the highest *trump* card. Aces are highest, then Kings, etc. down to the two's. However, the highest *trump* card played beats any other card from any other suit. Since Kyle dealt, he starts the play by laying any card from his hand into the middle. Every other player must lay a card in the same suit that he led. If a player does not have a card in that suit, he can either *sluff* a card of another suit or play a *trump* card. Then, once everyone has played one card for that hand, the person with the winning card takes the pile (keep in mind that any *trump* card beats the highest card of the suit that was led).

Steven won the first hand, so he places those cards to the side. He leads the next hand by laying another card; and play continues until everyone has exhausted his cards for that round. At the end of each round, players count how many hands they won. Players who won the same number as their bid receive ten points plus the amount of their bid. Since Kyle bid four and won four hands, he gets 14 points that round. Steven, however, went over the amount he bid, so he only gets points for the number of hands he won. Since he bid four but actually got five, he gets five points. Rachel bid six, but only won four hands, so she failed to attain her bid. In that case, she *loses* the amount she bid. Since she bid six, she loses six points. Megan bid zero and she didn't win any hands, so she earns ten points.

Rachel starts another round by dealing one card fewer than the previous round—the second round each player receives seven cards, and a new trump is determined. This repeats each round with the dealer dealing one less card each round until only one card is reached. Then the deal works back up—deal two cards, then three, etc. back to the original eight card deal. Once all rounds have been played, the player with the highest amount of points is the winner!

BIG BOOTY

 # OF PLAYERS: 4 or more
PLAYERS: Megan, Kyle, John, Rachel
OBJECTS NEEDED: Nothing

Players in this rhythm game sit in a circle, and each spot in the circle is numbered. The King spot is named "Big Booty," and then going to the left, the next spot is #1 spot, then #2, etc. around the circle for however many are playing. The object of the game is to stay on rhythm and work up to the "Big Booty" spot. To keep rhythm, players pat their thighs twice with their hands, then clap twice, then pat their thighs twice, and then clap twice, etc. (thus, there is a constant beat of four).

Megan is in the #1 spot, so she starts. On the two thigh pats, she says her number aloud, "Number 1," and then on the claps she says someone else's number. For example, on the thigh beats Megan says, "Number 1," and then on the claps she could say, "Number 4," or "Big Booty," or anyone else's number. If she said, "Number 4," then, Kyle, who is at spot #4, says his number and passes to someone else by saying another number. If a player does not stay on beat or makes a mistake, she goes to the end of the line and everyone else shifts up one spot. Play continues as players try to work their way to the "Big Booty" position.

VARIATION: To make the game competitive, players receive strikes for every time they make mistakes. In addition to moving to the end of the line, the player who made a mistake receives a strike, and three strikes eliminate that player from the game. In this version, being the "Big Booty" is not advantageous, the goal is simply to not make a mistake and stay in the game the longest to win.

VARIATION: Rather than having each spot assigned a number, each player chooses an animal, name, noise, sign, body movement, etc.

BUZZ

 # OF PLAYERS: 3 or more
PLAYERS: Megan, John, Rachel
OBJECTS NEEDED: Nothing

OR MORE

This game of numbers and speed is both challenging and a lot of fun! Players sit in a circle. Rachel begins by saying, "One." As she does this, she brings one of her hands across her chest and points to the next player. Whichever direction she points, that player says the next number, which of course is "two," and points in any direction to repeat the process. Players can point to the person on the left or the right, or even point across the circle to a random person. Whoever is pointed at, that player must say the next number and point in any direction within two seconds. The players continue counting upward to 100.

However, when the number "seven" is reached, or any number divisible by seven, that player must say, "Buzz." Play continues and the next person says, "Eight," then "Nine," etc. Any time a number has a seven in it, or is divisible by seven, that player must say, "Buzz" or she receives a strike. Thus, these numbers cannot be said: 7, 14, 17, 21, 27, 28, 35, 37, 42, 47, etc. up to 100. Players do not want strikes—three strikes eliminate the player from the game. Strikes are earned when players fail to say a number within two seconds, say the wrong number or fail to say "Buzz" at the appropriate time. Once the group reaches 100, start over at "one" again, but this time, rather than using seven as the "Buzz" number, use a different number (perhaps four and numbers divisible by four, etc).

VARIATION: For a greater challenge, have two "Buzz" numbers at once.

CARDS RELAY

 # OF PLAYERS: 4 or more
PLAYERS: John, Megan, Steven, Rachel
OBJECTS NEEDED: Deck of cards for each team

OR MORE

This relay card challenge can be played as a separate game or is often played as a *filler* game between rounds of other card games. The next time someone is reshuffling and dealing cards, try this quick team game!

Divide players into two teams. Give each team a deck of shuffled cards. For every round, each team completes a different pattern in relay style—players complete consecutive steps until the goal is accomplished. Patterns can be absolutely anything! For example, at "Go," each team races through their deck to pull out every card in a certain suit in numerical order. In our game, John and Megan race against Steven and Rachel to find every ♣ in order. John and Steven each begin by finding the 2♣, then John hands the deck to Megan and Steven hands his deck to Rachel. Megan and Rachel each find the 3♣, then hand the deck back to their partners. Play continues until all the ♣s are found. The first team to complete the relay receives a point.

Another example is finding the face cards for each suit. Each team finds the J♥ first, then the Q♥, then the K♥; then they'll move on to the next suit, etc. Another example is finding the Aces, the fives, and the Jacks for each suit—in that order. So, the first player has to find the A♥, then the next person finds the A♠, etc. Once all Aces are found, the next player finds the 5♥, then the 5♠, etc. Next, find the Jacks. Again, the first team to remove all of the right cards is the winner and receives a point. Another example is placing every card in descending numerical order, suit by suit. Thus, the first player finds the A♥, the next player finds the K♥, the next player the Q♥, etc. down to the 2♥. The next player then starts on the A♠, etc. down to the 2♠—repeating until every suit is in order.

Teams need to reshuffle between each relay race to maintain fair play. As a player tries to find the right card, he cannot help the next player by moving or rearranging cards. The team that scores five points first is the winner!

CHARADE DRAWING

 # OF PLAYERS: 4 or more
PLAYERS: Adam, Megan, Kyle, Sarah, Steven, John
OBJECTS NEEDED: Papers, Pencils, Bowl

OR MORE

If you're not a good artist, you'd better hope your teammates are great at guessing! To start, each player takes five slips of paper and writes various things: a famous person, a familiar place, a common object, a movie title, a song, an animal, etc. (it can be anything). Place all the papers in a bowl and divide the group into two teams. To begin, one person from each team comes to the front of the room. In our game, Megan and Sarah volunteer to go first. Since they'll be drawing clues, they choose one paper and look at it together.

Megan and Sarah return to their respective teams. When Adam declares, "Go," they each attempt to draw clues that will get their teams to guess what was written on the paper. When drawing, there is absolutely no talking by the person drawing, or writing letters or words to describe what is being drawn—*only* drawing is allowed. Each team races to guess what is being drawn. The first team that guesses correctly receives a point. Start another round by having each team send a new person to choose a slip of paper. This repeats until a team wins by reaching 15 points!

VARIATION: To make it more difficult, require the players to draw with their eyes closed.

COVERED TEETH COMPETITION

 # OF PLAYERS: 4 or more
PLAYERS: Adam, Kyle, Sarah, Megan
OBJECTS NEEDED: Nothing

OR MORE

This game may seem silly, but don't judge it until you try it—you will love it! Players sit in a circle and begin by covering their teeth with their lips. The object of the game is to keep your teeth covered for the entire game! If at any point someone's teeth show while talking or laughing, that person receives a strike. Two strikes eliminate the player from the game. Play moves clockwise around the circle and begins with a player saying, "Hello, my name is _____, I am wondering if you happen to have any _____." Players fill in the blanks with their names and with whatever they want for the second part of the sentence. The goal, of course, is to get your neighbors to laugh so that they show their teeth, but while doing so, not laugh yourself!

In our game, Adam began the game by turning to Kyle, who was seated on his left, and saying, "Hello, my name is Captain Obvious, I am wondering if you happen to have any aliens with green scales." Kyle responded by saying: "No, I do not have any aliens with green scales, but thank you for asking." (Note—players must respond in this manner.) Then, Kyle turned to Sarah to say, "Hello, my name is Dr. Botox, I am wondering if you happen to have any unattractive wrinkles." Naturally, Sarah almost cracked a smile, but managed to continue to play. It is important to note that even those not participating in the question/answer part still must keep their teeth covered. Thus, players receive strikes if their teeth show while talking or laughing, or if someone laughs so hard that she fails to respond to a question within five seconds. As the game continues, players with two strikes are eliminated and the person who keeps her teeth covered the longest is the winner!

CROSSWORD CATEGORIES

OR MORE

 # OF PLAYERS: 4 or more
PLAYERS: Rachel, Megan, Steven, John
OBJECTS NEEDED: Paper, Small Slips of Paper, Pencils, Bowls

....

This spin-off of *Scrabble*® is lively, interactive and competitive! Each person starts with four slips of paper and a pencil. On two of the slips, players write random categories, and on the other two slips they write eight letter words. Categories can be anything—countries, actors, athletes, famous people, clothing brands, company names, etc. For example, Rachel writes *Spain* and *Albert Einstein* on her category slips and *vigorous* and *accurate* on her word slips. They place the category slips and the word slips into different bowls, then divide players into pairs and give each pair a large piece of paper.

At the start of each round, someone chooses one word slip, and each pair writes the word horizontally across the middle of their paper. A category slip is

chosen for the whole group. At "Go," each pair has two minutes to think of words that relate to that category, quietly talk amongst each other, and write down words branching off the already written word. For example, when the category was *foods,* and the random word was *computer*, Steven's team wrote words related to foods that branched off the letters of *computer*. Branching off the letter *c* they wrote *cook*; off the *e* was *eat*; off the *m* was *meal*, etc. Then, from the words *cook, eat* and *meal*, his team wrote other food related words. Like *Scrabble®*, words go up, down or sideways—as long as they connect with other words, are actual words, and the letters of one word cannot be right next to another word.

At the end of two minutes, pairs compare their answers with the other pairs playing. A pair receives one point for each word they wrote that no other pair also wrote. Thus, if more than one pair wrote the word *meal*, neither receives a point. However, the pair that wrote the most words that other pairs did not write, receives an extra five points. Another round begins by choosing a different category and a new word. Play repeats until one pair reaches 50 points.

DIGITAL SCAVENGER RACE

 # OF PLAYERS: 4 or more
PLAYERS: Everyone!
OBJECTS NEEDED: Digital Cameras or Cell Phone Cameras, Cars

OR MORE

This scavenger hunt is a modern version of the old scavenger hunt. Divide players into two teams, or for larger groups, three or four players can be on a team. The entire group begins by brainstorming random things in the city/town that can be photographed. Items can be specific to the town or general things found anywhere—examples include a specific restaurant, a gas station, a railroad track, a movie theatre, a certain type of plant or tree, a McDonalds, a bumper sticker, a billboard, a child, a shopping cart, etc. (virtually anything will work). Give each player or team a list of the items, then determine whether teams have to find *all* the items on the list and be the first back to win or if there will be a time limit—after an hour everyone returns and the player(s) with the most items wins. Digital camera or cell phone pictures provide proof of the items "collected."

VARIATION: If there are not enough cameras, or players would rather participate in a traditional scavenger hunt, play using the same rules but send teams to collect designated random objects and/or accomplish random tasks. Examples include obtaining a fast food restaurant cup, getting a specific type of leaf, bringing back a smooth rock, running to and from the back wall of a grocery store, making four right turns on real streets, doing a Chinese fire drill in a parking lot, buying a random item at a discount store, etc.

DON'T SPELL A WORD

 # OF PLAYERS: 3 or more
PLAYERS: Kyle, Megan, Steven
OBJECTS NEEDED: Nothing

OR MORE

This challenging game tests your language skills. Someone begins play by saying any letter. Going around the circle, the person to the left says another letter, and the next person another, etc. The object is simple: don't be the person who completes the spelling of a word. However, each time players say letters, they need to have a legitimate word in mind. The word must be longer than three letters—a complete word that is only two or three letters long does not count. If, for example, the first three letters are *t* and *a* and *l*, then the next letter said cannot be an *l* or a *k* because that would be longer than three letters and complete a word (*tall* and *talk*).

When players say letters that complete words, they receive strikes—three strikes eliminate players from the game. There may be times when a player says a letter and the next person in the circle whose turn it is, doubts that the person before them actually had a legitimate word in mind. In this situation, the next player can challenge the person who just said a letter if she doesn't think that person had a legitimate word (one can only challenge the person right before them). If one challenges and is correct that the player didn't have a legitimate word, the person who didn't have a real word receives a strike. If someone challenges and the other player does have a legitimate word, the player who challenged receives a strike. Once a player receives a strike, or a word is spelled, the next player starts play with a new letter. This repeats until only one player is left—the winner!

VARIATION: There are six variations to this game—look in the *Children's Games* section under the game *Word Contests.*

DUEL OF WORDS

 # OF PLAYERS: 2 or more
PLAYERS: Adam, Rachel, Kyle
OBJECTS NEEDED: Papers, Pencils, Bowl, Timer

OR MORE

The hard part isn't thinking of words, it's thinking of words your opponents *won't* think of! Divide players into two equal teams. To begin, each person takes five small pieces of paper and writes down various categories—these categories are different word formations. For example, Rachel's categories include words ending in *th*, words that have more than four syllables, words with a double meaning, words with one syllable containing a double *s* or *t*, and words/adjectives ending with the letter *b*, while Kyle's categories include words ending in *our*, words with three of the same letter in the word, etc. Once everyone finishes writing five categories, collect the papers and place them into one bowl.

Play begins when a random player chooses a slip of paper from the bowl and reads it aloud. When the timer is started, the timekeeper says, "Go," and each team begins working together to write as many words that fit the criteria from the category/slip that was announced. Teams have 45 seconds to write as many words as they can. When the timekeeper says, "Stop!" at end of the 45 seconds, the teams receive one point for each word that no other team wrote. For example, if the category chosen was words ending in *our*, and two teams wrote *hour,* then neither team receives a point. The next round starts by drawing another slip of paper that determines the new category/criteria. Play continues until one team reaches 50 points.

EMOTIONS

 # OF PLAYERS: 4 or more
PLAYERS: Sarah, John, Steven, Megan
OBJECTS NEEDED: Papers, Pencils, Dictionary, Dice, Pennies

OR MORE

There are no teams in this game of *emotions*. Each person takes five slips of paper and writes five adjectives, adverbs, emotions, etc. John wrote *scared, quickly, emotionally, confused* and *joyfully*, while Megan chose *hyper, stressed, tired, nervous* and *skeptically*. All of the slips of paper are placed into a pile face down, then eight of them are turned face up, side-by-side (four on the top row and four on the bottom). The four spots on the top are numbered 1 - 4, and the bottom four spots are numbered 5 - 8. Each player takes a turn being the *emotional* reader, and the goal for everyone else is to correctly guess which emotion of the eight face-up emotions describes the reader.

Sarah begins by being the *emotional* actor—she rolls the dice without anyone else seeing. Since her roll is double threes, which adds to six, she must act a definition in the *emotion* that is located at spot #6. (Since there are two dice, players add the total of the dice to know which *emotion* to act. When the total equals more than eight, they simply roll again until the roll totals eight or less). Sarah then opens the dictionary to a random place, chooses any word and begins acting its definition in the *emotion* located at spot #6. For example, if spot #6 is *joyously* and she chooses the word *carnivorous*, she'll act the definition of *carnivorous* in a *joyous* way (acting helps *show/explain* the *emotion*).

The other players have ten seconds to decide what they each think the *emotion* is (this is done without talking or discussing—it is an individual guess). After ten seconds, at "Go," everyone simultaneously takes a penny and places it on the *emotion* spot they think is correct. Some pennies may actually be on the correct *emotion*, while other pennies may be on different *emotions* at other spots. The *emotional* reader receives a point for every player who guessed correctly and the players who correctly guessed the *emotion* receive a point, too.

After each round, replace the used *emotions* with new, unseen *emotions* from the pile (thus, the correct *emotion* and all the other *emotions* that people guessed are replaced with new *emotions* from the pile). Each person takes a turn being the *emotional* actor. The first person to reach 15 points is the winner!

FO' SHIZZLE MY NIZZLE

 # OF PLAYERS: 4 or more
PLAYERS: Kyle, Megan, Adam, Sarah
OBJECTS NEEDED: Nothing

OR MORE

The name of the game says it all—it is absolutely crazy and hilarious! Players sit in a circle. The object of the game is to pass specific noises around the circle while trying to get the person sitting next to you out. There are three specific noises made as the game progresses: 1) "Beep" 2) "Aaaahhhh" and 3) "Fo' Shizzle My Nizzle." Everyone initially starts on the noise "Beep." When players make mistakes, they progress to the next noise.

Kyle begins the game by saying, "Beep," while bringing his right (or left) hand across his chest and pointing to the next person. Since he brought his right hand across his chest (which meant he was actually pointing to his left), the noise passes to the person on his left—Megan. Megan can pass the noise in whatever direction she wants. She says, "Beep," as she points and passes the noise to Sarah. Sarah can either point to the left or reverse directions to send the noise back to the right.

The goal is to move the noise quickly without making a mistake. There are two ways to make a mistake. First, if a player is on the noise "Aaaahhh," for example, and he mistakenly says, "Beep," that is a mistake and he moves to the next noise. Secondly, if a player says her noise and points out of turn, she moves to the next noise. Mistakes happen because the noise moves around the circle and changes direction quickly, plus players intentionally try to throw people off. All players begin on the noise "Beep," but after a mistake, the mistaken person switches to "Aaaahhh" the next time the noise comes back. As the game progresses and people start making mistakes, some remain on "Beep" while others are saying "Aaaahhh." A second mistake changes that person's noise to "Fo' Shizzle My Nizzle." When a player makes a mistake whose noise is "Fo' Schizzel My Nizzle," that third mistake means he is out of the game and must sit silently and watch until the next round starts. The last two people remaining receive a point. Play continues until someone scores three points to win!

VARIATION: Try the sounds: Beep, Bop and Bang. Whenever someone passes to the left, she says, "Beep," while still passing the motion by pointing in one or the other direction. Whenever someone passes to the right, he says, "Bop." To mix it up, a player can say, "Bang" and point to a random player in the circle. The motion goes to the person pointed at and he says either, "Beep," or "Bop," or even "Bang." If a person does make a mistake, he receives a strike, and after three strikes, he is out.

FOUR ON THE COUCH

 # OF PLAYERS: 8 or more

PLAYERS: Adam, Rachel, Kyle, Megan, Steven, John, Sarah, Anna

OBJECTS NEEDED: Papers, Pencils, Bowl

OR MORE

This team game may seem easy the first round, but each round gets more confusing, difficult and fun! Write the names of each player on small slips of paper and place the slips into a bowl. Each player draws a slip from the bowl. It is okay if someone draws her own name, however, players must not tell anyone whose name they chose. Players sit in a circle (on couches, chairs, the floor, etc.) around the room, but leave one extra spot empty. If, for example, there are eight people playing, there needs to be nine spots around the circle—one spot always remains empty. Since this is a game of remembrance, if someone forgets her drawn name or the drawn name of another player, the other players (teammates included) cannot tell the correct name.

The goal and object of the game is to get your team onto the "hot spot"— the four spots on the couch (or other designated area if no couch is available). There are various ways to establish teams: boys against girls, boy names vs. girl names drawn, or designate random teams of four people (by actual people or by drawn names)—but there does need to be four on a team.

To begin, the person to the left of the empty seat calls a random name (keep in mind that nobody knows each other's drawn name at this point). Whoever drew the name that's called (not the actual person in real life) moves to the empty spot. Thus, a new spot becomes empty, and the person to the left of that new empty spot calls out another name. This continues, and players slowly start to discover who is who...but the trick is to remember the new names of your teammates (and the opposing team's names') so that when you need to move someone to or from a specific spot, you can call the right name. Once an entire team is on the couch, they win that round. To start another round, everyone draws a new name and switches teams. This is where it gets fun! Just as players begin to feel confident in the names from the last round, they have to remember people by completely different names, plus who their new teammates are, etc.

VARIATION: To make this game competitive and keep points, teammates remain together each round. Thus, it could be girls vs. boys; however, each round, each player still draws a different name. The first team to win three rounds is the winner.

GROCERY STORE ABC GAME

 # OF PLAYERS: 4 or more
PLAYERS: Anna, Sarah, John, Steven
OBJECTS NEEDED: Papers, Pencils

OR MORE

This entertaining game is perfect for a date night, teens or group of friends, or even for the kids. Divide those playing into pairs and go to a local grocery store. Each pair starts at the front of the store with a paper and pencil. The goal is for each pair to find a product for every letter of the alphabet, write down a product that no other pair does, and be the first team back to the front of the store. Pairs only receive points if they write down a product that no other team wrote down. Speed is essential since the first team back to the starting position earns an extra ten points.

At "Go," each pair scatters throughout the store to search for products for each letter of the alphabet. The letter has to come from the first letter of the product, and it has to be the brand or label name. So, for example, a pair can't use "B" if they see a banana—they would use "D" for Dole because Dole is the banana's brand name or company/product. Also, pairs can use "S" for a Snickers, but not "C" for a candy bar. They can use "C" for Colgate, but not "T" for toothpaste, etc. Pairs have to write down the letter, the brand name they found for that letter (only one product can be written), and the aisle they found it on (to prevent cheating). Then, the first pair back to the front gets an extra ten points. Once all pairs are back to the front of the store, everyone compares answers, and again, pairs only receive points for products/brands that no one else put on their list. The pair with the most points wins the game.

GUESS THAT MOVIE

 # OF PLAYERS: 4 or more
PLAYERS: John, Kyle, Rachel, Adam, Megan, Steven
OBJECTS NEEDED: Paper, Pencil, Bowl, Timer

OR MORE

Everyone quotes movies all the time—but acting them out creates a great competitive game! Each player takes four slips of paper and on each slip records a scene from a popular movie—everyone playing should be familiar with them. Players should initial their own slips to identify the source of each movie scene. Divide those playing into two teams and place the slips of paper in a bowl. In our game, John, Kyle and Rachel are playing against Adam, Megan and Steven. John's team volunteers to act first.

John chooses a slip of paper from the bowl. He does not reveal to anyone what is written on the paper, but he announces the initials of the person who wrote it since that person is not allowed to guess as the scene is acted. After about 15 seconds of thinking what to do, at "Go," John has 30 seconds to act the scene for his team. This is done without talking, writing letters or words, or pointing to things—only acting is allowed! His teammates have 30 seconds to guess the movie correctly—if they do, they receive one point. Adam's team then takes a turn by choosing a slip from the bowl and having one of their teammates act the new movie scene. This repeats until one team wins the game by scoring 15 points!

VARIATION: Rather than just one person, have two teammates come to the front and act the scene.

VARIATION: Each person (or pair) has one minute to act as many scenes as possible. Once the team correctly guesses the first scene, another slip is drawn and acted, repeating as many times as possible in one minute. Teams receive a point for every scene acted and correctly guessed in that time.

HEARTS

 # OF PLAYERS: 4 or more
PLAYERS: Adam, Rachel, Kyle, Megan
OBJECTS NEEDED: Deck of Cards

OR MORE

....

Four people play this game at a time, but more players can rotate into play since rounds are quick. To begin, deal the entire deck evenly between the four players and have them organize their hands by suit. The person to the left of the dealer starts by playing any card. The three remaining players must play a card in the suit that was led. For example, when a ♠ is led, every other player must lay a ♠ card. If a player does not have a card in the suit that was led, then she can play any other card. The person who played the highest card in the suit that was led wins the hand and places the cards at her side.

Winning a hand is only important when there are "point" cards in the hand. In this game, players do not want points! Point cards are as follows: every ♥ card is worth one point. The only other card in the deck that is worth points is the Q♠—it's the card everyone is trying to avoid because it is worth 15 points! For example, if Adam wins a hand with two ♥ cards in it, he receives two points. If Q♠ was also in that hand, he would receive 17 points (15 + 2). If Rachel actually wins every point card in a round—called a flush—then she gets zero points and the other three players each receive 20 points. At the end of each round, every player tallies the number of points won. Simply deal again to start another round. The first player to reach 100 points loses that round. Of the three other players, the person with the lowest amount of points when the first person reaches 100 points receives one point for winning that round (this is a *good* point). If more than four people would like to play, rotate players in by having the new player replace the person who just lost. The first person to win three points (full rounds) is the winner!

HOW WOULD YOUR PARTNER ANSWER?

 # OF PLAYERS: 4 or more
PLAYERS: Sarah & Steven, Rachel & Adam
OBJECTS NEEDED: Paper, Pencils, Bowl

Partners can be anyone—a spouse, boy/girlfriend, parent, sibling, friend, cousin, etc. To begin, each person takes five small slips of paper and writes random questions intended to discover certain things about another player. The questions can be anything. For example, what is...one of your dreams, your favorite movie, your biggest pet peeve, your favorite band, your most embarrassing memory, etc. Place the questions in a bowl and give each partnership a paper and pencil.

One person from each partnership leaves the room—Sarah and Rachel in our game. While they are gone, three random questions/slips are chosen. Steven and Adam write what they think their partner's answers will be. Since one of the questions asked was the player's favorite movie, Steven writes *Ever After*, since he thinks that is Sarah's favorite movie. When everyone returns to the room, one at a time those who left are asked the three questions. They respond aloud to the whole group, and then their partners reveal what they guessed. Each partnership receives one point for each correct match. Once everyone who left the room has answered, the other partner from each partnership leaves the room and three new questions/slips are drawn. This repeats round after round. The partnership that scores 20 points first, or has the highest score at the end of a designated amount of rounds, wins!

I HAVE NEVER...

 # OF PLAYERS: 6 or more
PLAYERS: Megan, Steven, John, Sarah, Anna, Adam
OBJECTS NEEDED: Nothing

Players sit in a large circle, with one spot *less* than the number of players.

One person starts by standing in the middle of the circle and saying, "I have never _____." The player can fill in the blank with anything, but it has to be true (no lying in this game). After the player says what they HAVE NOT done, all of those sitting in the circle who HAVE done what the person in the middle has NOT done must stand up and run to find an empty spot (which was created by an opening from another person who also got up to run). The player in the middle also scrambles to an open spot. Upon reaching an empty spot, players sit down leaving one person stranded in the middle without a seat. This person then resumes play by saying, "I have never _____."

For example Megan began by saying, "I have never been skydiving." All of the players who had skydived rushed for new seats. Since John didn't get one fast enough, he moved to the center and said, "I have never had a child." After the mad rush, that time Anna was left in the middle. She said, "I have never been to Alabama..." Play continues until people are ready to begin a new game.

VARIATION: The game can also be played by saying the opposite, "I HAVE _____," then all those that HAVE NOT done that must rush for an open seat.

VARIATION: To make the game competitive, players receive one strike for each time they become the person in the middle. Once a person is in the middle three times, she is out. The last two people playing are the winners.

VARIATION: If players would rather not run around, give everyone three pennies. If they HAVE done something or NOT done something (depending on which version you are playing), players throw in a penny to the middle *ante*. Once a player is out of pennies, he is out. But, if someone is the only person in the room who HAS or HAS NOT done something, he or she wins all the pennies in the *ante*.

IMPROMPTU TEAM CHARADES

 # OF PLAYERS: 6 or more
PLAYERS: Adam, Rachel, Kyle, Megan, Steven, John, Sarah, Anna
OBJECTS NEEDED: Papers, Pencils, Bowl

Players divide into pairs. Each pair takes three slips of paper and together they write down various random things people do. Examples include eating at a restaurant, cheering at a baseball game, driving in traffic, reading a magazine at a bus stop, grocery shopping, waiting at a doctor's office, etc. Once everyone has written three things, place all the slips into a bowl.

One pair begins play by selecting a paper/situation from the bowl. Working together, they act the situation for the rest of the group. When a slip is drawn, the pair only has 10 seconds to begin acting—there cannot be any speaking, collaborating or planning before they start. Impromptu acting is what makes this game fun! The pair has 30 seconds to act the scenario, while all the other pairs try to guess what situation they are portraying. To keep everyone from shouting guesses, each pair should designate a spokesperson. The pair that correctly guesses first receives a point, plus the acting pair receives two points if another pair correctly guesses within the 30 second time limit. This creates incentives to both act well and be the first to guess the situation correctly. After 30 seconds, if no other pair has guessed correctly, nobody gets any points. Each pair rotates, taking turns being the impromptu actors. The first team to score 20 points wins the game!

INCHYPINCHYWINCHY

 # OF PLAYERS: 4 or more
PLAYERS: Megan, John, Sarah, Anna, Kyle
OBJECTS NEEDED: Lipstick

Some games can be stupid, but a whole lot of fun at the same time! This is not a game people play often—it is a "prank" game to play the next time a friend, neighbor or relative comes to visit who has a good sense of humor and has never played the game.

Players sit in a circle around the room. The person who has never played before is referred to as the *victim*. The person sitting to the right of the *victim* needs to have some lipstick. In this case, John is the victim and Megan is sitting next to him. She rubs a small amount of lipstick on her finger, and then hides the lipstick so John cannot see it. Everyone else keeps a straight face—no one can laugh, snicker or stare!

The game starts when a random player, Sarah, turns to the person on her left and with her index finger she does some random thing to the face of her neighbor. While doing this, she says, "Inchypinchywinchy." Examples of random motions include pinching a cheek, rubbing a nose, squeezing a chin, pulling an earlobe, drawing a line on her forehead, etc. Sarah turns to Megan and gently pinches her cheek. Neither Sarah or Megan laugh nor smile—they just pretend it is part of the game. The random motion only needs to last a few seconds, but neither person can laugh. If a player does laugh, she receives a strike (three strikes and a player is out of the game). It is important that the rule is enforced to make the *victim* think this is an actual game (as weird as it may seem to them). Part of the fun is being more lenient on the *victim* so that he isn't eliminated from the game.

Play continues around the circle. Since it is Megan's turn, she pinches John's cheek with the finger that has lipstick on it—thus smearing it on John's face. The person rubbing lipstick on the *victim* must be very subtle and not let the *victim* see the lipstick. Each round the victim's face becomes funnier. Players laugh and receive strikes until the game ends when the *victim* finally discovers what is going on!

 # OF PLAYERS: 4 or more

PLAYERS: Kyle, Rachel, Adam, Anna

OBJECTS NEEDED: Paper, Pencils, Two Bowls, Timer

OR MORE

Players need eight small pieces of paper apiece—on six pieces they write categories and on two pieces they write words with four letters (no swearing!). Place all the category slips of paper into one bowl and all the words into another bowl. The categories can be anything that can be acted—sports, movies, famous people, animals, places, etc. Divide players into teams of two or three players and give each team a large piece of paper.

To begin, Kyle chooses four category slips from the category bowl and grabs one word. Kyle tells the entire group what the four categories are, as well as the word. Each team takes their piece of paper, and on the left side of the paper, they write the four categories vertically along the page. They then write the four letters of the word horizontally along the top of the paper (thus forming four rows and four columns). At "Go," each team collectively thinks of and writes a word for each category that starts with the first letter of the word written along the top.

	W	I	N	K
SPORTS	Water-polo	Ice Skating	Netball	Karate
FAMOUS PEOPLE	Walt Disney	Indiana Jones	Neil Armstrong	Kelly Clarkson
ANIMALS	Walrus	Iguana	Nilgai	Kangaroo
PLACES	Wisconsin	Indiana	New York	Kabul

Since Kyle chose the four-letter word *wink*, each team's paper has W I N K written across the top. His first category is *sports*, so each team thinks of sports that start with the letters "w," and "i," and "n," and "k." His next category is *famous people*, so teams use the word W I N K and think of a *famous person* for each letter. At this point, Rachel's team paper reads: "**W**aterpolo, **I**ce Skating, **N**etball, **K**arate" on the *sports* line, and "**W**alt Disney, **I**ndiana Jones, **N**eil Armstrong, **K**elly Clarkson" on the *famous people* line. Play repeats for all four categories. Teams have one minute to complete as many of the 16 boxes as possible. After the one-minute time limit, each team receives one point for each completed box. If Rachel's team only filled in 10 boxes, her team receives 10 points, etc.

But, this is where the game gets fun! Now, each team will take a turn and will have to act 2 of the words/boxes they completed. Rachel's team may decide to act Karate and Neil Armstrong, for example. Taking turns, each team sends one person to the front to act their two words (players from each team take turns being the actor for different rounds). No talking is allowed while acting. Players have 45 seconds to act both words. As soon as the first word is guessed correctly, they quickly start on the next word to try to act it within the 45 seconds. Players from the opposing teams are trying to be the first to correctly guess what is being acted, and the first team to guess receives a point. The person acting also has an incentive to act well because his team receives a point if both words are guessed within the 45 seconds. After the 45 seconds, or the two words are guessed, the next team sends someone up to act their two chosen words, etc.

Once each team has acted, teams will tally all their points (how many boxes they filled in plus the points they earned by guessing and acting). Start another round by choosing four new categories and a new word. Play continues until one team has reached 100 points and wins!

KING OF THE DICTIONARY

 # OF PLAYERS: 3 or more
PLAYERS: Rachel, Megan, John, Anna
OBJECTS NEEDED: Dictionary, Papers, Pencils

OR MORE

Who said dictionaries can't be fun? There are no teams in this game. Select a *King* and rotate each round so that everyone takes a turn being the *King*. In our game, Anna is the first *King*. Anna starts by opening the dictionary and choosing a random word that most people would NOT know. The word chosen is irrelevant—the harder the word, the better. The other players write their own definitions of the chosen word. The goal is to make every definition sound so convincing that other players will think it is the real meaning of the word. Anna (the *King)* writes the correct definition of the word on her paper.

Players hand their definitions to the *King*. Anna reads all the definitions aloud for everyone to hear. After hearing the definitions once (sometimes twice), players vote on which one they think is the correct definition. When a player guesses correctly by voting for the *King's* definition, he receives a point. In addition, each player receives a point for each vote his definition won—a great incentive to write a definition so well that others will vote for your imaginary definition. When a player actually does know the chosen word's real definition and writes it correctly, that is worth an additional three points (in addition to those earned when other players vote for the definition). Players take turns being the *King* and choosing a word, and the first player to reach ten points wins!

MAFIA

 # OF PLAYERS: 10 or more
PLAYERS: Everyone!
OBJECTS NEEDED: Nothing

OR MORE

Be prepared for a brutal game of "killing" and "lying"—and also to have a lot of fun! A narrator is chosen to moderate the game. To begin, the narrator asks the players to close their eyes. The narrator then chooses two people to be the *Mafia*, two *detectives*, and the remaining players are *citizens*. While everyone's eyes are closed, the narrator lightly taps the head of the two chosen to be the *Mafia* and taps the shoulder of the two chosen to be the *detectives*. This method ensures the *Mafia* won't know who the *detectives* are, and the *detectives* won't know which players are *Mafia*.

While everyone's eyes remain closed, the narrator asks the *Mafia* to open their eyes. Together the *Mafia* selects one person to be "killed." The *Mafia* players should be silent and still to protect their identities as they make their selection. They indicate their choice by quietly pointing at a person—and it can be anyone. The *Mafia* then closes their eyes again, and the narrator asks the *detectives* to open their eyes. They, too, should be quiet and still so they are not discovered. The *detectives* now guess who they think might be one of the *Mafia*—no talking allowed, they simply point to one person. The narrator indicates whether the person they guessed is *Mafia* by silently indicating yes or no. The *detectives* close their eyes and the narrator asks all the players to open their eyes so that play can begin.

Although nobody knows who is who at first, the *detectives* and *citizens* are on the same team. Their mission is to find the *Mafia* and "kill" them. The *Mafia's* mission is to kill all the *detectives* and *citizens*. To begin, the narrator informs everyone whom the *Mafia* killed while everyone's eyes were closed. (The narrator can add some fun by making up a story about how the person died.) Then the floor is open to discussion and accusations as the players try to discover the *Mafia's* identities. While it is hard at first, players want to find "evidence" to prove why they think a certain player is *Mafia*. After a few minutes of conversation, certain people will become the target of accusations because of various reasons (often silly and illogical at first).

After roughly three to five minutes of discussion, the narrator conducts a vote to determine who should be "killed." If there is more than one accusation, then after everyone votes, the majority wins. At this point, the person who received the most votes gets to give a dying testimony trying to convince everyone else that he is innocent (yes, players may have to lie!). A final vote is held. If the person's argument was persuasive enough to change the vote, then he stays in the game and the discussion and accusations begin again. If "killed," that player reveals his status (*Mafia, detective* or *citizen*)—and for the remainder of the game he is "dead," which means he has to remain silent, cannot participate and must not reveal anything to others still playing.

Round two begins and the process repeats—players close their eyes, the *Mafia* selects someone to "kill," the *detectives* guess who they think the *Mafia* might be, then the narrator informs everyone who died, and the floor again opens to discussion and accusations, etc. As each round continues, things start to be revealed and discoveries made—other players may have great evidence or reveal who they are (possibly lying) to try and "kill" others, etc. Players die as rounds progress. Since the object of the game is for the *Mafia* to "kill" everyone and be the last ones standing, if one or both of the *Mafia* members remain alive at the end—the *Mafia* wins. The opposite is also true—if only citizens and detectives are alive at the end, they have won by killing off the *Mafia!*

MYSTERIOUS PLACEMENT

 # OF PLAYERS: 4 or more
PLAYERS: Anna, Kyle, Steven, Sarah
OBJECTS NEEDED: Pencil, 9 books or magazines of the same approximate size

OR MORE

This game requires patience and may get a little frustrating as everyone tries to discover the *trick*! In preparation, place nine books or magazines on the floor very close together—arrange them three rows by three columns. To begin, two people need to know the *trick* before the game starts—one person is the *pointer* and the other is the *guesser*. In our game, Steven is the *guesser* so he leaves the room and the rest of the group chooses one of the nine books. The goal is for everyone to figure out *how* the *guesser* knows exactly which book the group chose when the *pointer* (Anna) points to the correct book.

After the group chooses a book, Steven returns to the room. Anna starts randomly selecting books one by one, and asks Steven, "Is this the book the group chose?" Steven replies, "No" until the right book is chosen. How does the *guesser* know? Because he agreed beforehand that the *pointer* would point to a certain place on each book when she asks, "Is this the book the group chose?"

Imagine the covers of each book broken into a 3 x 3 layout similar to the way the nine actual books are placed on the floor. For example, if the *pointer* always points with the pencil to the top right portion of a book—the *guesser* knows that the actual book the group chose is the book in the top right corner of the 9 books on the ground. If however, the *pointer* always points to the middle section on a book, the *guesser* knows it is the middle book, etc.

When the *pointer* does point to the chosen book, the *guesser* confirms it is the correct book. After the successful guess, everyone wonders how the *guesser* identified the right book. The two who know the *trick* continue to repeat the steps—the *guesser* leaves and the group chooses another book. After a few times, others playing start to catch on and think they know the *trick*. At this point, when a player thinks he knows what the trick is, he doesn't reveal it to the group—instead he proves it by leaving the room and becoming the *guesser*. If he returns and correctly identifies the book the group chose when the *pointer* points to it, he keeps the *trick* a secret. Such a player can either sit and watch or help by being the *pointer* or the *guesser* again while others try to figure out the *trick*. Play continues until everyone has discovered what the *trick* is.

VARIATION: A suggestion to avoid embarrassment if people cannot figure out what the *trick* is—divide players into groups of two or three and then have it become a race to see which team can decipher the *trick* first.

NOUN GAME

OR MORE

 # OF PLAYERS: 6 or more
PLAYERS: Anna, Sarah, John, Steven, Megan, Kyle, Rachel
OBJECTS NEEDED: Nothing

Begin by asking three people to leave the room—we asked Steven, Megan and Rachel to go. The remaining players choose three things to act: a *person*, a *place* and a *thing*. These "nouns" can be anything—any *person*, *place* or *thing*. One of the three who left the room returns—the two players who left stay in the other room where they can't see or hear the game. Steven chooses one person from the group in the room to act the *person*. After this, Steven will choose a different person to act the *place*. Then Steven will choose another person to act the *thing*. Without talking, these three actors only get 30 seconds and they can only act each thing once. After all three *nouns* have been acted, Steven still does not guess what he thinks each *noun* is.

Megan now returns, and Steven acts out each *noun* (the *person*, *place* and *thing*) to her. Again, no talking and only 30 seconds is allowed to act each *noun*. Megan does not guess what each *noun* is, but must act the *nouns* to Rachel. After Megan acts all three *nouns*, Rachel guesses what each *noun* is. Then, start another round and send three different people out of the room, and this repeats.

VARIATION: Play this game as teams and keep track of points. Divide the group into two equal teams, and each team takes turns sending three teammates out of the room. When the third player correctly guesses a noun, that team earns a point. The first team to 10 points is the winner!

PASS THE MESSAGE

 # OF PLAYERS: 8 or more
PLAYERS: Everyone!
OBJECTS NEEDED: Papers, Pencils, Bowl

Each player writes a random word on three small slips of paper. The words can be absolutely anything. Place all the words in a bowl, then divide players into two teams. To begin, one person from each team goes to the front and each pulls out three slips of paper. Sarah and Adam look at the words and have approximately 20 seconds to incorporate them into a brief story. The story can be random, but it must include the three words and should only take between 20-30 seconds to tell.

Sarah and Adam each choose a player from the opposing team and they all leave the room. While gone, Sarah and Adam each quietly tell their opponents the 20-30 second long story they made up. When sharing the story, the goal is to say the three words discreetly so the other player doesn't know which words in the story are important.

Everyone returns to the room and the players who heard the story whisper it (as quietly as possible and as best they can remember) to the next teammate. That teammate then whispers the story to another teammate, etc. until everyone on the team has heard a version of the story. When the last person on each team hears the story, he tells it to the entire group. The goal is for the final version of the story to include as many of the original three words as possible. For each word that makes it through the entire process, the team receives one point. Play continues as different players from each team choose three new words, etc. This repeats until one team has scored 20 points to win the game!

PERFORMANCE CHAIN

 # OF PLAYERS: 6 or more
PLAYERS: Everyone!
OBJECTS NEEDED: Papers, Pencils, Bowl, Timer

If you are going to be embarrassed acting, you might as well have some company! Each player takes six slips of paper and writes the names of three *famous people* and three common *situations*. The *famous people* can be anyone, as long as players would know/recognize the person. The *situations* can also be any familiar thing. The *situations* our players wrote included mowing the lawn, at the grocery store, at the dentist, doing the laundry, putting makeup on, playing a video game, etc. Place all the slips of paper for the *famous people* in one bowl and the slips of paper for the *situations* in a separate bowl. Lastly, divide players into two teams and select a player to act as timekeeper.

The first team begins by sending three teammates to the front of the room. When the timekeeper says, "Go," *Player 1* grabs a slip from the *famous people* bowl and without talking, acts the *person* to *Player 2* (of the three teammates at the front). Only *Player 2* can guess the *person* that *Player 1* is acting. Once *Player 2* guesses the *person* correctly, she grabs a paper from the *situation* bowl and acts that *situation* out to *Player 3*. Once *Player 3* guesses the *situation* correctly, he goes back to the *people* bowl and acts a *person* for *Player 1*. This continues for one minute. Each team's goal is to act/guess as many people and situations as possible within the time limit. Teams receive one point for every correct guess (keep in mind that a team does not guess, only the *players* at the front acting make guesses). The next team takes a turn doing the same thing. The action continues until a team reaches 30 points to win!

PERPLEXING LINGUISTICS

 # OF PLAYERS: 6 or more
PLAYERS: Adam, Rachel, Kyle, Megan, Steven, John, Sarah, Anna
OBJECTS NEEDED: Nothing

OR MORE

Divide players into teams of two to three people. At the start, two people (*Player 1* and *Player 2*) secretly agree on a verbal *pattern*. *Player 1* begins the game by saying a word (any word) to *Player 2*. After doing this, *Player 1* tells

Player 2 that she is thinking of another word, and then asks Player 2 to tell her what that word is. Player 2 tells Player 1 the correct word. Then, Player 2 thinks of another word and asks Player 1 what word she is now thinking of. Player 1 knows what that word is, and tells Player 2. This repeats back and forth, confusing the other players as they wonder what the pattern is. The goal is to be the first team to discover the pattern.

In our game, Megan and Anna are Player 1 and Player 2 and Megan chose the word cook. The secret pattern they both know is that each subsequent word will start with the last letter of the previous word. Therefore, Anna can choose any word that starts with a 'k.' Anna chooses the word king since she knows the word really does not matter, as long as it starts with the same letter as the last letter used in Megan's word. Megan now chooses a word starting with the letter 'g,' etc. Play continues until one team discovers, or thinks they have discovered, the pattern. When a team thinks they know the pattern, they join the conversation to prove that they really do know the pattern. However, each teammate on the team must prove she knows the pattern. The first entire team to discover the pattern receives five points. At this point, the winning team does not reveal the pattern since the 2nd team to discover the pattern receives three points and the 3rd team receives one point, which ends that round of play. The first team to score 20 points is the winner!

After a round ends, the winning team thinks of a new pattern. Anything is possible—just use your imagination! Below are a few our players chose:

- Player 1's words end with a 't' while Player 2's words end with an 'e.'
- Answers that varied between a particular noun sequence—person, place and thing.
- The first letter of each answer spells a word (if the word is talk, Player 1's word starts with a 't,' then Player 2's word starts with an 'a,' etc.).
- The first letter of Player 1's word must be the last letter of Player 2's word.
- Player 1's words are three letters long and Player 2's words are four letters long.

VARIATION: Linguistic Brainteaser. Player 1 says, "I like books, but not novels." Player 2, who knows the trick—that the first word said has a double letter in it and the second word does not—replies, "I've been to Mississippi, but not to Iowa." Other examples might be, "I feel happy, but not sad" and "I am little, but not large," etc.

VARIATION: Numerical Confusion. Two players know what the *secret* is—one of them is the *mind reader* and the other is the *narrator*. The *mind reader* leaves the room. While he is gone, the group chooses any number. When the *mind reader* returns, the *narrator* calls random numbers—and the *mind reader* knows exactly which number the group chose when the *narrator* says that number. The question is—how? Let's say, for example, that the number the group chose was 57. The *narrator* then asks the *mind reader*, "Is the number 43? ... 461? ... 7? ... 57?" At this point the *mind reader* knows it is 57—because the first number the *narrator* said was '43.' The very first number was the number '4' ... which told the *mind reader* that the number the group chose would be the 4th number the *narrator* says. The team that scores 20 points first is the winner! Examples of *secrets* that can precede the right answer include:

- The number that follows any number ending with a '7'
- A number with all even numbers in it; a number that is divisible by 5
- Any number that starts with a '1'

VARIATION: Map Psychic. Place a map or globe in the center of play. Two players start knowing what the *trick* is—one is the *map psychic* and the other is the *narrator*. The *map psychic* leaves the room, and while she is gone the group collectively chooses a random city anywhere on the map. Once a city is chosen, the *map psychic* returns and the *narrator* starts naming random cities. The *map psychic*, of course, knows exactly which city was chosen when the *narrator* says that city. How? The *map psychic* knows the *trick*. For example if the *trick* is that the chosen city always follows a city with two words in the name, then if the group chooses the city of *Chicago*, the *narrator* asks the *map psychic*, "Is it Miami? ... London? ... Mexico City? ... Chicago?" The *map psychic* knows Chicago is the right answer because it followed the first city with two words (Mexico City) that the *narrator* said. *Tricks* can be anything—examples include:

- It is the city that follows a city name that starts with the letter A.
- The city that follows a city named in South America.

- The second named city after a city with two identical letters next to each other in the city name (Mississippi, Pittsburgh, etc.).

The remaining teams try to discover the new *tricks* and play continues until one team scores 15 points to win!

PSYCHIATRIST

 # OF PLAYERS: 4 or more
PLAYERS: Anna, Megan, Rachel, Kyle, Steven
OBJECTS NEEDED: Nothing

OR MORE

A little patience and intelligence are required for this tough mind game—it can take some time! To begin, two players leave the room so they cannot hear or see the others. While they are gone, the other players collectively think of a pattern they will use to answer questions. Once a pattern is chosen, the two players return. Their goal is to ask questions that will help them discover the pattern. The questions they ask are irrelevant, they can literally ask anything—it's the answers that are important. As the two ask questions, everyone answers according to the predetermined pattern. Once they figure out the pattern, two new people leave the room. The game continues with the group choosing a new pattern. Sample patterns include:

- Everyone answers as if he/she were one of the other players.
- Partners answer each other's questions (this requires remembering what they asked the partner).
- The first letter of the first word in the reply spells something.
- Each person who answers starts his first word with a consecutive letter (the first person would use A, the next person B, etc.).

VARIATION: For an easier variation of this game, instead of choosing a pattern, everyone chooses an object and a place (a 'what' and a 'where') for where these two are and what they are doing. The two people try to ask questions to discover where they are and what they are doing.

VARIATION: Another easier way to play is to have everyone choose a "taboo letter." Perhaps the taboo letter chosen is "M"—then the answers cannot have *any* words containing the letter "M." If someone says the taboo letter in an answer, that person receives a point—players do not want points in this version since three points knock a player out of play for that round. The winner is the last remaining player. Rotate and take turns being the person who leaves and guesses.

VARIATION: Rather than choose a group pattern, each *player* has a pattern. When the guessing player leaves the room, everyone else shares their pattern with the group. When the person who left comes back in, rather than asking the group or people randomly, she goes around the circle asking each person one question to discover that individual's pattern. Once the person guessing discovers and guesses a player's pattern, that person is out for that round. The player who remains in the round the longest receives a point. Everyone takes turns being the guesser and the first person to three points is the winner! Sample individual patterns include:

- Not actually answering the question asked.
- Answering as if you are someone else.
- Answering someone else's question.
- Always saying a color in your answer.
- Scratching your face each time you are asked a question
- Mentioning a food or place.
- Beginning each answer with a cough.
- Using a number in your answer.
- Incorporating a lie into your answer.

RECKLESS DRESS UP

OR MORE

 # OF PLAYERS: 6 or more
PLAYERS: Everyone!
OBJECTS NEEDED: Blindfold and articles of *old* clothing: shirt, pants, socks, gloves, hat, shoes, coat

Some games are competitive and require strategy, while others are just for fun—this is one of them! Divide players into two teams and give each team a pair of mismatched gloves, a blindfold, a funny hat, a shirt, a large coat, a pair of baggy pants, a pair of old socks and mismatched shoes. Place each team's clothes in a separate pile at one end of the room. At "Go," a player from each team races to the team's pile, places the blindfold on, puts on the two gloves first, and then puts on every other article of clothing. Once a player is wearing everything, he takes the blindfold off, quickly takes off all the clothes, and rushes back to tag the next player on his team. In relay race style, the next player rushes to the pile and repeats the process. The first team to finish wins!

VARIATION: Rather than being blindfolded, each player must keep a balloon in the air by bouncing it while dressing. The goal is to keep the balloon from touching the ground, so every time the balloon does touch the ground the team receives a point (ask a player from each team to keep track of the other team's score). It is still a race however, because the first team finished subtracts five points from its score—the team with the lowest score at the end of the relay is the winner!

VARIATION: Play the same game, but do it outdoors in relay race style. Each team has its own pile of clothes at the starting line. The first player must put all the clothes on, run to a line about 30' away, and then return to the finish line to tag the next teammate. As the first player is taking the clothes off, the next player is putting them on. This repeats until one team wins the relay.

SCUM

 # OF PLAYERS: 4 or more
PLAYERS: Steven, Anna, Sarah, Rachel
OBJECTS NEEDED: Deck of Cards

OR MORE

Steven begins by dealing all the cards in the deck evenly to players. Players arrange their cards in ascending numerical value. The goal is to be the first to get rid of all of your cards. Steven starts by playing any one of his low cards. Anna plays a card that either matches or is higher in value than the card just played. If Steven played a three, Anna can either play a three or any other higher card. Play continues around the circle with each person playing a card from any suit, as long as it matches or is higher in value than the card previously played.

Since Sarah does not have a higher or matching card, she passes for her turn, and play moves to Rachel. Even if a player *does* have a higher card, he can choose to pass and not play the higher card—a strategy to reserve a higher card for later in the round. Twos are the lowest and Aces are the highest, but that does not mean that a two has to be the first card played, or that an Ace will always be the last card played. (For example, after everyone passes, a ten may be the highest card, or a King). Regardless of what the last card is, once everyone has passed, the person who played the highest card clears the center cards and starts another hand. This person can play any card, or cards, he wants. For example, he can play a two, or a ten. He also can play double or triple cards (two 3s, or three 8s, etc.)—then everyone else must lay a matching or higher set of doubles or triples for that hand.

The first player to get rid of all of his cards becomes the *King* for the next round. Play continues until all the cards have been played. The next person to play all her cards is in the #2 position; and this continues down to the last person with cards in his hands—that person becomes the *Scum* for the next round. At this point, everyone rearranges seats so that they are sitting in order—*King*, 2nd position, etc. down to *Scum*. The *Scum* has to shuffle the cards and deal; however, in addition, once players look at their cards, the *Scum* also has to give his two highest cards to the *King*, and the *King* in exchange gives the *Scum* her two lowest cards (the *Scum must* give his two highest cards). Also, the person who is in the 2nd position, exchanges one card with the person next to the *Scum* (one highest for one lowest). Each round that a player remains the *King* (she has to *win* as the *King*), she receives one point. The first player to score five points is the winner!

SHEER DECEPTION

 # OF PLAYERS: 2 or more
PLAYERS: John, Sarah, Adam
OBJECTS NEEDED: Deck of Cards

Often referred to as *BS,* this extremely fun game allows players to "lie," "cheat" and "deceive" in order to win! The goal is to get rid of your cards the quickest—even if takes "lying" to accomplish it. To begin, deal all the cards evenly to each person playing. The dealer starts and plays a two of any suit. The player to the left plays a three, the next person plays a four, etc. However, as cards are played, they are placed face down so that nobody sees what cards were played. Players must play a card on their turns regardless of whether they have the right card or not. For example, if the card to be played is supposed to be an eight, and Adam doesn't have an eight, he can play any other card as long as he doesn't get caught! At least one card must be played on each turn.

Play rotates in numerical order from twos up to Aces. More than one card can be played on a single turn, and players announce what cards they're playing as they place the cards on the table. For example, as John plays his card, he says, "One three." Then Sarah says, "Three fours," etc. If Adam suspects that Sarah has lied, he can challenge her. Anyone can challenge, but if the challenger is wrong, that player must pick up all the cards in the discard pile! If the player who challenged is right (the person *did* lie), the person caught lying must pick up all the cards in the discard pile. Once the discard pile has been picked up, play resumes with the next card in the sequence. The first player to get rid of all of her cards wins that round and receives one point. The person who reaches three points first wins the game!

SIGNS

 # OF PLAYERS: 6 or more
PLAYERS: Adam, Rachel, Kyle, Megan, Steven, Anna
OBJECTS NEEDED: Nothing

Everyone sits in a large circle with one player (*it*) standing in the middle. In our game, Anna is *it*. Players begin by choosing their individual signs. Examples of signs include blinking one eye, crossing legs, touching an ear, yawning, scratching an elbow, bobbing head, picking nose, etc. Those seated pass their signs secretly back and forth trying to keep *it* from finding where the sign is. Anna closes her eyes and counts to ten to give the players in the circle time to start passing signs. Adam starts by doing his sign, and then passes to Rachel by doing her specific sign. All the players must be discreet—they must watch the sign as it is passed in a way that won't reveal to *it* who has the sign.

Rachel accepts the sign by doing her specific sign, and then she passes it to Kyle by doing his unique sign. For example, if Rachel's sign is a yawn, and Kyle's sign is a wink, Rachel will yawn and then wink. Now, Kyle will wink, and then do someone else's sign, etc. As Anna is searching for the sign, players can wait or stall to accept or pass signs so *it* does not see, but players have to pass the sign within 30 seconds once the sign comes to them. Whoever is caught by *it* with the sign becomes the new *it* in the middle.

VARIATION: Rather than each person choosing a sign, designate each chair in the circle with a sign that stays with that spot. For example, spot 1 might be a yawn, spot 2 a blink, spot 3 crossing legs, etc. When a player becomes *it*, the old *it* goes to the last spot in the circle, and everyone moves up one spot. The goal is to get to the #1 spot since players receive a point for every time they remain in that spot. Each time a new person becomes *it*, a point is given to the person in spot #1, unless he was the one that made a mistake. The first person to reach 10 points wins the game!

SLAMMERS & CREEPERS

 # OF PLAYERS: 4 or more
PLAYERS: Megan, John, Sarah, Kyle
OBJECTS NEEDED: A quarter

OR MORE

You'll discover how much fun you can have with just a quarter in this rambunctious game! Divide players into two teams. This game is played at a table with each team sitting on opposite sides of the table facing each other. Team A goes first by having everyone on the team hide their hands under the table as they pass a quarter between themselves. This continues for roughly 30 seconds until a player on Team B says, "Stop!" All the players on Team A then place their closed fists on the table so Team B can't see which player has the quarter. Team B then tells Team A to either do *Slammers* or *Creepers*. Team A must simultaneously (as best they can) do *Slammers* or *Creepers*.

If *Slammers* is chosen, the entire team must slam their hands onto the table at the same time. The goal is to not let the quarter fall or be seen when everyone slams their hands. Yelling and making noise is allowed to prevent the opposition from hearing the quarter hit the table. If *Creepers* is chosen, teammates slowly and silently creep their hands onto the table—trying not to let the other team hear or see the quarter. Now, Team B has to guess which player's hand is hiding the quarter. They get two guesses to choose correctly, but instead of choosing a person, they choose one hand at a time. If Team B finds the quarter by the second hand chosen, they receive a point; if not, Team A receives a point. Play continues with Team B passing the quarter under the table and Team A choosing *Slammers* or *Creepers*. This repeats until one team reaches 10 points and wins the game! [Note: This game should *not* be played on tables that are easily scratched or damaged.]

VARIATION: To make the game a little more difficult, secretly pass one quarter and two pennies. As *Slammers & Creepers* are being done, the opposing team may hear coins, but the goal is still to find the quarter by the second guess. If they choose a hand with a penny, it does not count, but if the guessing team finds the quarter by the second guess, they receive a point.

SLAP THE DECK

OR MORE

 # OF PLAYERS: 3 or more

PLAYERS: Adam, Megan, Sarah

OBJECTS NEEDED: Deck of Cards

Card rules are as follows:

- Jacks and 10s—Slap the Deck
- 2s—Reverse Play
- 5s—Skip a player
- Aces—Wild
- Kings—Choose any player to pick up one card

Begin by dealing eight cards to each player, placing the remaining cards in a center pile. The player to the left of the dealer begins by playing any card (forming a discard pile), and play continues around the circle to the left. For example, if a 3♥ was played first, the next player can play any ♥ card, any 3, or an Ace (wild). If a player cannot play a card in the middle, his turn is drawing a card from the middle pile.

The goal is to be the first to get rid of all the cards in your hand. When any 2 is played, the direction of play reverses. When any 5 is played, that player can choose one person to skip the next turn. All Aces are wild—they can be any card or change suits. A person who plays a King can choose any player to pick up one card. Whenever any Jack or 10 is played, it is a race to "Slap the Deck." The player who plays the Jack or 10 must literally Slap the Deck and say, "Slap the Deck!" Everyone else then must Slap the Deck—the last person to Slap the Deck must pick up all the cards in the discard pile and add them to her hand. Play continues until one person gets rid of all his cards, thus earning one point. Reshuffle, deal again and start another round. The first person to three points wins the game!

SOLITAIRE BATTLE

 # OF PLAYERS: 2 or more

PLAYERS: Rachel, John

OBJECTS NEEDED: Deck of cards for each player

OR MORE

....

Each player takes her own deck and deals 13 cards in a pile face down, and then turns over the top card. Players then place four cards face up side by side in a horizontal row beside the pile of 13 cards (referred to as the *four piles*). The remaining cards are held face down in each player's hand.

Players race against each other to be the first to discard their entire deck of cards the quickest. At "Go," players start placing their cards into four separate discard piles in front of them, and each player has her own four discard piles (these separate piles are referred to as the *discard piles*). A discard pile must begin with an Ace. For example, once the A♥ has been played, only the 2♥ can be played on top of the A♥; then the 3♥, etc. all the way up to the K♥. Eventually the four Aces in the deck will be played and players continue to lay cards on their four discard piles in ascending order from Ace up to King.

A player can play a card onto one of her four discard piles by playing the top face up card of her pile of 13 cards, or from one of her *four piles*. If a player cannot play from one of these two methods, she takes the top card from the pile of 13 and places it onto one of the *four piles* (she turns over the next card from the pile of 13). However, the card from the pile of 13 can only be placed on a card one higher in value, but from any suit. Thus, the cards on these four piles are added to in descending order as the round progresses. Keep in mind that like *Solitaire*, the beginning card from one of the four piles may not be a King—it could be a 5, but the next card to be played on that 5 has to be a 4, then a 3, then a 2, which would end that pile. Then, if a player still cannot play any card onto one of her four discard piles, she turns over one of the cards from her hand. This card can be played to the center, or onto one of the four piles. If this card also cannot be played, it is placed to the side and another card from her hand is turned over until she can go (once all the cards in a player's hand have been played or placed to the side, the player takes the cards placed to the side and starts over trying to play them again).

When a player does play a card from one of her four piles onto one of the discard piles, she can only play the last card played (or the top card from that pile). So, in the pile with the 5, 4, 3 and 2 card—the 2 card must be played onto a discard pile before the 3 card, etc. If a player removes a card that depletes one of her four piles, a new pile is started by replacing it with one card from the pile of 13 cards (this pile of 13 depletes as the game progresses). Play continues in this manner, and the first player to play every card onto her four discard piles (thus the Ace to the King in every suit has been played), wins that round and receives a point. Reshuffle, deal again and start another round. The first person to score three points is the winner! (Just like normal *Solitaire*, it is possible for a player to get stuck where none of her cards will play).

SPEED

 # OF PLAYERS: 2 or more
PLAYERS: Anna, Rachel
OBJECTS NEEDED: Deck of Cards

OR MORE

While this game of speed has only two players at a time, others can rotate in and out since the pace is very fast. Begin by dealing the entire deck of cards between the players. Place two cards in the center face down by each other, then to the side of each of the two cards place a pile of 10 cards each face down. Lastly, deal the rest of the cards face down evenly between the players. Each player takes five cards from her own pile (not the piles of 10 in the center) and holds them in her hand.

Play begins by flipping over the two cards in the center. The goal is to be the first person to get rid of her entire pile of cards by discarding any of the five cards in hand onto one of the two piles in the center. Only cards that are one higher or lower than the card on top of the center pile can be played. For example, if the top card of one pile is a 5, Anna or Rachel could play either a 4 or a 6 on top of the 5. As they play their cards onto the center piles, they replenish their hands by drawing more cards from their piles, thus keeping five (and only five) cards in their hands at all times.

In the event neither player can play a card onto the two center piles, they simultaneously take cards from the piles of 10 cards to the sides of the center piles. At the same time, they flip over one card until one of them can play a card onto one of the center piles. Play continues until one player has played every card in her pile—she receives a point. If more people are playing, others rotate in and the winner stays to challenge the next person. The first player to score five points wins the game!

SPEED GUESSING

 # OF PLAYERS: 4 or more
PLAYERS: Kyle, John, Steven, Anna, Rachel, Megan
OBJECTS NEEDED: Papers, Pens, Bowl

OR MORE

20 Questions is a game for kids...*Speed Guessing* is a game for adults who are quick, competitive and want to have fun! Divide players into two equal groups. Each player writes random nouns on 3 to 5 small pieces of paper—famous people, places, countries, sports, animals, foods, objects, etc. Fold the papers and place them all in a bowl. Each team sends one teammate to the front of the room to draw a slip of paper. These two players show the slips of paper to the opposing team—not their teammates—to prevent teams from cheating. The goal is to be the first to guess what's on your team's slip of paper. In our game, the guys are battling the girls and John and Rachel were the first to choose slips of paper.

Kyle begins by asking John one question in an effort to discover what is written on the paper. Although any question is fair, the answers can only be

Yes or *No*. After the first team asks a question, the next team takes a turn. Keep in mind that each team is trying to discover its own word—not the same word. Play continues with alternating teams asking one question at a time until one team correctly guesses the right word. A guess counts as the team's turn. Since teams are limited to five guesses per round, part of the strategy is carefully using guesses. A correct guess earns the team one point per round. Play continues with another player from each team drawing a slip and answering questions. The first team to score 10 points is the winner.

SPELLING MANIA

 # OF PLAYERS: 4 or more
PLAYERS: Adam, Rachel, Sarah, John
OBJECTS NEEDED: Dictionary

OR MORE

You may be able to spell...but can your teammates? Divide players into two teams. The first team begins by randomly selecting a word from the dictionary for the other team to spell. Rather than choosing an extremely hard word, teams should choose words that are tough to spell but not extremely difficult since the opposing team will undoubtedly match or escalate the difficulty. The other team attempts to spell the word correctly, then it is their turn to choose a word for the first team to spell. Play goes back and forth between the teams based on one of the variations discussed below. When a team spells the word correctly, they receive a point. The first team to reach 15 points wins the game!

VARIATIONS: There are many ways to play this game. They include:

- Teammates take turns spelling consecutive words. For each new word, a new teammate attempts to spell that word.
- The entire team spells the word together. The first player on the team says the first letter, the second player says the next letter, etc. (Once a letter is said, no corrections are allowed.)

- The team collaborates quietly and one person acts as the team spokesperson to spell the word.
- Teams collaborate to spell the word backward in one of the formats listed above.

SPIT

 # OF PLAYERS: 2 or more
PLAYERS: Kyle, Anna, Steven
OBJECTS NEEDED: Deck of Cards

OR MORE

This fun, challenging card game is played with two people at a time. Other players can rotate in since games are relatively fast. After all the cards are dealt evenly between the players, players set up their cards in front of them as follows:

1) Place four cards side by side in a horizontal line in front—three cards face down and the last face up.
2) Place a card face down on the first two cards and a card face up on the third—leave the fourth card as is.
3) Place a card face down on the first pile and a card face up on the second pile of cards.
4) Place a card face up on the first pile only.

Players place their remaining cards face down next to the four piles in front of them. To begin, both players say, "Spit!" and immediately flip the top card on their spare piles face up into the center next to their opponent's card. Players then try to play the face up cards from their four piles onto one of the two cards in the center. Players can only play a card into the center if it is one higher or lower than the card showing—if a 9 is one of the cards in the center, only a 10 or an 8 can be played.

Once someone plays a face up card from one of his four piles onto one of the two center cards, he turns over the next face down card in that pile. Players continue to play their cards into the center until neither player can move. When that happens, both say, "Spit!" as they take the top cards from their spare piles and place those two new cards face up on the center piles. Play continues unless neither player's card plays—in that case, the players keep saying, "Spit" and turning over new cards until one plays. (When players run out of cards in the spare piles, they simply turn over the discard piles and use those when neither can play.) The first player to play all the cards in his four piles wins that round and receives a point. If more players are playing, a new player rotates in to challenge the winner. The first player to score three points is the winner!

SPOONS

 # OF PLAYERS: 3 or more
PLAYERS: Megan, Steven, John, Adam
OBJECTS NEEDED: 2 Decks of Cards, Spoons

OR MORE

Shuffle two decks together, deal four cards to each player and place the remaining cards in a pile in the middle. Next to the middle pile of cards place the spoons—one spoon *less* than the number of players in the game. The first goal is to collect four of a kind, or four cards of the same value (four 6s, or four Kings, etc). Once someone has collected four of a kind, she grabs a spoon—the next goal is to be one of the players to grab a spoon.

The dealer, Megan, starts by picking up a card from the middle pile. She decides if she wants that card or not and then discards a card she doesn't want (or isn't collecting) by placing it face down for the person on her left—Steven. Steven picks up the card that was passed to him, decides whether to keep the card or not, then discards one card to the player on his left. Play continues until someone collects four of a kind—John is the first with four 6s. John grabs a spoon (grabs can be very discreet or very fast!). Once he grabs a spoon, the race is on—everyone else tries to get a spoon before they're all gone. Since Adam didn't get a spoon, he receives one strike. Two strikes knock a player out for that round. Whenever a player is knocked out, one of the spoons is removed, the cards are reshuffled and play starts again. The player who is still in when everyone else receives two strikes gets one point. The first player to score three points is the winner!

VARIATION: To make the game even more fun, place the spoons in another room, outside or upstairs. When someone gets four of a kind and takes off, everyone else is in a mad rush to get to the spoons the fastest. Be careful!

STRATEGIC WAR

 # OF PLAYERS: 2 or more
PLAYERS: Rachel, John
OBJECTS NEEDED: Deck of Cards

OR MORE

Two people play this card game at a time—simply rotate other players in since play is quick. To begin, deal the entire deck face down evenly between the two players. Without looking at their cards, each player chooses 10 random cards and places them face down in a horizontal line. Players hold their remaining cards in their hands.

Play begins with both players choosing a random card from the cards in their hands. They play the chosen cards into the middle at the same time. The person with the higher numbered card gets to take both cards and place them in a winning pile. Players choose another random card, and the person who has the higher card wins those cards. Keep in mind that suits are irrelevant—a 5 beats a 4, a King beats a Queen, Aces are highest, etc. *But 7s beat every other card!*

While it may seem like this game is pure luck, there is some strategy to the madness. If, for example, Rachel plays a lower card, she can *challenge* her opponent. To *challenge,* Rachel chooses one of her 10 cards, flips it over and plays it into the middle. If her challenge card is higher, she wins all 3 cards, but if it is not higher, she loses all three cards. Even if she challenges and wins, John can challenge her back. If a 7 gets challenged, any higher card value above a 7 beats a 7 in a challenge. Challenges can keep going until someone stops challenging, but players only have 10 cards to challenge with for the entire game. The game is won when a player wins all the cards, has the most cards when time is called, or has the most cards when both people run out of challenge cards.

STRATEGICALLY LUCKY

 # OF PLAYERS: 2 or more
PLAYERS: Adam, Sarah, Megan, John
OBJECTS NEEDED: Deck of Cards

OR MORE

Play begins by dealing four cards face down to each player—these four cards remain face down, laying side by side in a horizontal row in front of each player. The dealer then deals eight more cards to each player (use 2 decks if necessary), and the players look at these eight cards and place any four of those cards face up on top of the four face down cards—players have one face up card atop each of their four face down cards. Players keep the remaining four cards in their hands. The leftover cards are placed in a pile in the center, face down, with one card flipped over to form a discard pile.

The object of the game is to be the first player to get rid of all of his cards. To begin, players work collectively to deplete the center pile. Then, each player tries to get rid of his own cards in this order:
- Get rid of the four cards in his hand.
- Get rid of the four cards face up in front of him.
- Get rid of the four cards that are face down beneath the four face up cards.

The player to the left of the dealer, Sarah, begins by playing a card onto the discard pile that is higher than the value of the top card. If a 5 is showing, Sarah must play any card (from any suit) that is higher than a 5 (and she can only play a card from the four cards in her hand). The next player, Megan, plays a card that is higher than the one just played. For example, if Sarah played a 9, then Megan must play any card that is higher than a 9 (Aces are high). At the start of the game, when a player discards a card, he picks up a card from the draw pile to keep four cards in his hand at all times. If, however, a player cannot play a card that is higher, he must pick up the entire discard pile and add those cards to his hand. This continues around the circle.

In addition to the above rules, certain cards also have certain rules:

- 2s are wild—they act as any number/face card.
- 6s reverse play—the direction of play switches when a 6 is played.
- 7s require the next person to play a lower card value rather than a higher card value (a card lower than a 7).
- 8s allow the player to skip any player's next turn.
- 10s clear the pile—take away the discard pile and place it to the side so no player adds those cards to her hand.

Once the center draw pile is depleted, players work to get rid of the four (or more) cards in their hands—they must play the cards in their hands before choosing to play to the center any one of the four face up cards. If he cannot play any of those cards, he must pick up the discard pile, get rid of those cards, and *then* get rid of his face up cards. Thus, as the game progresses, a player may actually have only one more face up card to play to the center, but if he can't play that card, he must pick up the discard pile and then get rid of those cards before he plays his last face up card.

Once a player has played all his face up cards, he attempts to get rid of his four face down cards. With these cards, a player cannot flip them over to look at them. For each turn at this point, a player randomly chooses one of his face down cards to play to the center. If that card is higher, he is lucky. If it is lower, he must take the discard pile and again have to play the cards in his hand before playing his face down cards again. The first player to get rid of all her cards receives a point. Reshuffle, deal again, and the first person to get three points is the winner!

TEAM SPELLING COMPETITION

 # OF PLAYERS: 4 or more
PLAYERS: Sarah, Megan, Adam, John, Anna
OBJECTS NEEDED: Dictionary, Papers, Pencil

OR MORE

This game requires teamwork, a quick mind and fast fingers! Divide the players into two equal teams. In preparation, write each letter of the alphabet four times on small pieces of paper (each letter is on four different slips of paper). Spread all the letters on a table, face up, and be sure they are mixed up well. Send one player from each team to the table. An independent person (one who is not on any team) randomly chooses a word from the dictionary—in our game it is Anna. Anna should choose a mixture of words—some familiar but long words, some difficult words and some easy words. Once she chooses a word, Anna says it aloud and the players at the table from each team race to spell the word correctly as fast as possible. The two competing players from each team must spell the word using the pieces of paper on the table by lining up the papers with the letters in the proper order and place. The player who spells the word the fastest receives a point for his team.

If the person at the table doesn't know how to spell a word correctly, she can get help from her teammates. Teams can help in three ways:

- Only one person from a team can speak to the teammate at the table.
- A team is limited to two helpful suggestions each round.
- A team's response can only be one letter at a time.

For example, if Adam is at the table struggling to spell a word correctly, he may turn to his team for help or suggestions—but he must ask his question in such a way that the team's response is just one letter. His teammates can talk back and forth amongst each other about how to spell the chosen word as long as he cannot hear them. The team's spokesperson responds with a single letter answer. For example, Adam could ask, "Should the *I* or the *E* be first?" or "What comes after the *T*?" etc. Teams can only say something if and when the player at the table requests help.

The first player at the table to spell the word correctly receives a point for his team. If both players are stumped and both teams have exhausted their two questions, then each team gets one chance to spell the word collectively. Both teams write the spelling of the word they think is correct—if both are right, then both teams get a point; if both are wrong, then no team gets a point. Start a new round by having another player from each team go to the table with letters on it, etc. The first team to score 10 points is the winner!

THE NUMBERS RACE

OR MORE

 # OF PLAYERS: 4 or more
PLAYERS: Adam, Rachel, John, Kyle, Anna, Megan
OBJECTS NEEDED: Paper, Pencils, Timer

Divide the group into two teams. Each team needs to prepare two sets of flash card pages—these are simply sheets of paper with the numbers 0 - 9 written on them. Next, ask every player to write 10 simple mathematical problems on 10 small slips of paper (one problem per slip). The answer to each math problem must be only one or two digits and the correct answer should be written on the back of the slip of paper. Sample mathematical problems include:

- What is 34 + 18?
- What is 98 - 13?
- What is 6 x 7?
- What is 42 ÷ 7?

Place the finished slips in a large bowl. To start, each team sends two players to the front of the room. Each player will hold one of the 0 - 9 flash card page sets. A random person (not one of the players at the front) pulls one slip from the bowl and reads the mathematical question to the group. Once the question has been read, the four people at the front race to be the quickest team to answer the question correctly! Players must provide answers in the following way:

- When the answer is only one digit, any of the players can answer by pulling out the right flash card page with the proper number on it and holding it up.

- If the answer is a two-digit number, both teammates must work together. One teammate holds up the first number, while the other teammate holds up the second number of the answer.

Both speed and accuracy are important since the team that holds up the most correct answers in each round receives a point. Once a team answers a question correctly, the person asking the questions reads another mathematical question—these rapid-fire questions continue for one minute. If in the one minute time period, Team A answers four questions the fastest, while Team B only answered two questions the fastest—then Team A receives a point for that round. Play continues with each team sending two different teammates to the front until one team reaches 10 points to win.

VARIATION: To make this game much more difficult, increase the difficulty of the math problems. Teams need a few more papers with numbers on them, and the two players at the front need to hold multiple papers depending on the answer. Using a calculator helps ensure the answers written on the back of the slips are correct. Teams may use a paper and pencil to compute answers if needed. Since these answers take longer to compute, increase the time limit to two minutes for each round. More challenging questions include:
- What is 2,457 + 479?
- What is 9,456,321 - 4,567?

TOURNAMENT OF INTELLIGENCE

 # OF PLAYERS: 4 or more
PLAYERS: Rachel, Kyle, Megan, Steven, John, Sarah
OBJECTS NEEDED: Paper, Pencils, Bowl, Coins

OR MORE

Divide players into teams of 2 - 3. Players designate 10 categories. Examples of categories include:

- Historical facts and dates
- The singer of a certain song
- The main character's real name from a certain movie
- Questions on anatomy
- The name of an athlete who holds a certain record
- The capital of a country
- The scientific name of a flower
- The answer to a mathematical question
- A state's capital

Each team writes various questions from the 10 categories on 10 slips of paper. The questions should be factual and objective, somewhat challenging, but not extremely difficult. Specific questions created by each team remain with that team.

A large piece of paper creates a playing board. Simply draw about 30 boxes (about 1 x 1 inch) in a consecutive line (use two pieces of paper if necessary). Teams use a coin to mark their position as they advance from the starting box to the last box.

Team A begins by reading one of their 10 questions to the remaining teams. Each team writes their answer to the question asked on a sheet of paper. Teams have 30 seconds to quietly discuss and write down their answers. After the 30 seconds, the team that read the question reveals the correct answer. A correct guess moves the team's coin ahead one space on the playing board. Teams take turns asking their questions, and play repeats until one team has moved across all 30 boxes to reach the last box and win!

TRAPS

 # OF PLAYERS: 3 or more
PLAYERS: Adam, Kyle, Megan, Anna
OBJECTS NEEDED: Deck of Cards

OR MORE

To begin, deal 10 cards to each player and place the remaining cards in a center pile (use two decks for larger groups). The player to the left of the dealer begins by playing a card in front of himself (it can be any random card from his hand). The next player can either play any card in front of herself or play a card beside the card played by the previous player. In order to play a card beside another card, it must be one number higher or lower in value than the card that was played—a 4 can only be placed by a 3 or a 5, and a Queen can only be placed by a King or a Jack, etc.

The goal is to complete and collect as many *traps* as possible. A *trap* is when a player places a card by another card and *traps* it. For example, if a 4 is played next to a 3 and someone either plays a 5 next to the 4 or a 2 next to the 3, a *trap* is completed. The person who completes a *trap* takes the *trap*—the *trapped* card and the two cards that surrounded it— and places those three cards to the side.

A player is only allowed one discard pile in front of herself, and *only* she can start a pile in front of herself. Once this card has been played, she cannot play another card on it—she must play a card on another player's pile. However, if a *trap* removes this pile, she can start a new pile (remember— players cannot start piles for other players). Thus, a player cannot obtain a *trap* from the cards in front of herself. If a player cannot discard one of her cards, and she already has a pile in front of her, she must pick up a card from the middle pile for her turn and she cannot play that card. The goal is to be the player who gets rid of all of her cards the quickest. The first person to get rid of her cards receives three points, and the next person to get rid of his cards receives one point. After that, reshuffle and start another round. The first person to score 20 points is the winner!

TRIVIA BASKETBALL CHALLENGE

 # OF PLAYERS: 4 or more
PLAYERS: John, Steven, Megan, Kyle
OBJECTS NEEDED: Trivia questions, Paper, Nerf® ball, Bucket

OR MORE

Who said trivia is only intellectual—now it's competitive and athletic! Divide players into two teams. In preparation, spend a few minutes creating or compiling some objective questions about geography, history, sports, religion, entertainment, etc. As an alternative, use the trivia questions from a board game, or have each player write factual trivia questions on three slips of paper and write the answers on the back. Since the player who wrote a question is not allowed to answer when it is chosen, players should also write their names or initials on each slip. Place the trivia questions in a bowl.

Team A begins by drawing a question to ask Team B. Team B has 30-40 seconds to collaborate and answer the question. If Team B answers the question correctly, they get a point. Team B then draws a question to ask Team A. When a question is answered correctly, the game has a little twist and becomes much more fun.

Set up a bucket or small garbage can in the room against a wall, and designate a shooting line about 10' to 15' from the bucket. After a correctly answered question, one player from that team throws the ball from behind the line to try to get it inside the bucket. Each player from each team takes turns being the shooter. If the shot is made the team earns an extra 2 points in addition to one point for the correct answer. The team that reaches 20 points first is the winner!

VARIATION: Try bowling! Set up 10 plastic cups approximately 10' to 15' from a designated line—place the cups in a normal bowling pin formation (4 in the back row, then 3, then 2, then 1). Players roll a ball to try to knock over the cups. Teams get one throw per try, receive one point for every cup knocked over, and five extra points for a strike! The first team to score 100 points is the winner!

TWO TRUTHS & A LIE

 # OF PLAYERS: 3 or more
PLAYERS: Sarah, Kyle, Adam, John
OBJECTS NEEDED: Nothing

The object of this fun game is to *lie* and score lots of points doing it! To start, players think of two truths about themselves or things they have done in their lives and then make up one lie. They write the truths and the lie on a piece of paper. The goal is to lie so well that the others playing do not know which of the three statements is the lie. The truths and the lies can be completely random—in fact, the more random the better when playing with people who know each other well.

Players gather in a circle and take turns reading their truths/lies aloud to the group. After each person has read his own truths/lie, everyone takes a group vote to determine which statement is the lie. Players who correctly guess by voting for someone else's lie receive a point. After each person has read his truths/lie, start another round by having each person write another set of truths and a lie. The first person to score 10 points is the winner!

ULTIMATE

 # OF PLAYERS: 4 or more
PLAYERS: Adam, John, Steven, Kyle
OBJECTS NEEDED: Deck of Cards, Paper, Pencil

Deal the entire deck evenly to players, but place at least 5 cards to the side. Players arrange their cards by suit and in descending order. Point values are as follows:

- Aces = 5 points
- Face cards = 3 points
- 10s = 1 point
- 5s = -1 point (minus one point)

Before play begins, players determine what they will bid based upon how many points they think they can win. Each player bids according to how many hands he thinks he can win. The dealer bids first. For example, he may start by bidding 20 points. The player left of the dealer either passes or bids higher. If a player passes, he is finished bidding for that round. Bidding continues until one player bids the highest and wins the bid. The player who wins the bid gets to take the extra cards and choose which five they want to keep and discard five cards they do not want. In addition, the person who wins the bid gets to call the *trump* for that round. *Trump* is the suit that beats any other card played from another suit during that round—even a 2 of the *trump* suit beats an Ace of any non-*trump* suit.

The dealer starts the round by playing any card he wants to lead. Starting to the left of the person leading, each player in turn plays a card in the same suit that was led. If a ♥ was led, players must lay a ♥ if they have one. If a player does not have a card in the suit that was led, he can play another card from any suit—including *trump*. The person who played the highest card wins the hand—the highest card is either the highest in the suit that was led or the highest *trump* card played. The person who wins the hand places the cards to his side and leads another card to start the next hand.

The goal for the person who won the bid is to win enough hands with point value cards to reach his bid. However, the object of the other players is to prevent the bidder from making his bid by winning hands with point value cards. After all the cards have been played, players total the points they won (keep in mind that each 5 card *deducts* one point). If the winner of the bid does make his bid, he receives as many points as his bid and the other players do not receive any points. However, if the bidder fails to make his bid, all the other players get half the point value of what he bid (thus, there are incentives to stop the winning bidder and to risk winning the bid). After everyone's points are recorded, deal again to begin another round. Play continues until one person reaches 150 points.

VARIATION: Call Your Partner. The person who wins the bid chooses a partner, if desired. After winning the bid he calls for someone with a card he needs to make his bid. He may say, "My partner has the Ace of Hearts." The player with the called card doesn't reveal himself until he plays the specified card, but secretly helps the winning bidder get as many points as possible. The two work as a team to try to win the bid. If they succeed, each receives points for the winning bid.

VERBAL LIMITATIONS MATCH

 # OF PLAYERS: 4 or more

PLAYERS: Adam, Anna, Rachel, John, Steven

OBJECTS NEEDED: Paper, Pencil, Bowl

Each player should take 10 slips of paper and write answers for each of the following categories:

- Famous person
- Movie
- Song
- Actor
- Country
- Food
- Subject
- Sport
- Clothing article
- Animal

Place all the papers into a bowl and divide players into two teams. One person from each team goes to the front. In our case, John and Steven are the first players. Together the two choose one slip from the bowl and look at the word. Their job is to describe the word to the group. The first team to guess what is on the slip of paper earns a point. Players are not allowed to say what category the word falls into or the word or any portion of the word. Most importantly, each player can only say one word at a time, and both players alternate saying words!

If, for example, the word chosen is *banana,* John starts by choosing one descriptive word about a *banana* to say—*yellow.* Steven chooses the word *fruit.* They alternate back and forth saying one descriptive word at a time until someone guesses *banana.* Although teams are allowed to guess after their teammate says a descriptive word, they only have three guesses per word. If a team uses its three guesses and fails to guess right, the other team can still guess and try to get a point (unless they, too, fail to guess correctly three times, which means that word is done).

When a team correctly guesses the word, it receives one point. Once a word is guessed, the two at the front draw another word and play continues. The two remain at the front until five words have been guessed, then a different player from each team comes forward. This repeats until one team has reached 30 points.

VOCABULARY RACE

 # OF PLAYERS: 4 or more
PLAYERS: Megan, John, Anna, Kyle
OBJECTS NEEDED: Paper, Pencils, Bowl, Timer

OR MORE

Even players with a vast vocabulary falter under pressure! Each player writes random categories on three slips of paper. Categories could include countries, movies, occupations, names, sports teams, cities, famous people, etc. In preparation, write the letters of the alphabet on individual slips of paper. Place the categories in one bowl and the alphabet letters in a separate bowl. Divide players into two teams (for larger groups form multiple teams of three players).

To start, one player goes to the front of the room and chooses a category and a letter. In our game, Megan goes first. At "Go," she informs the group of the chosen category and letter. Each team has 30 seconds to write down as many things as possible in that category that start with the chosen letter. If, for example, the category is *occupations,* and the letter is *A,* then teams write as many *occupations* as possible that start with an *A.* After 30 seconds is over, teams compare answers. A team receives one point for every *occupation* listed that no other team listed. Thus, if two teams wrote *attorney,* neither team gets a point for that word. A new player chooses another category and letter to continue play. The first team to 50 points is the winner!

VARIATION: Each round, choose several categories and have teams write the chosen categories vertically along the left side of the team's paper. Then, with the letter chosen, teams list as many things as possible using that letter in each category listed vertically along the paper. Teams have 1-2 minutes for this variation and receive a point if they list something another team did not list.

WHATEVER YOU DO—DON'T SMILE

 # OF PLAYERS: 4 or more
PLAYERS: Adam, Rachel, Kyle, Anna
OBJECTS NEEDED: Paper, Pencils, Bowl

OR MORE

Grab your poker face, throw out your sense of humor, and just try to keep from grinning! Divide the group into two teams. Players should write five different funny actions or settings on five slips of paper and place them all in a bowl. Virtually anything can be funny—here are a few examples:

- Pretend you are a child or an elderly person
- Act a funny movie scene
- Make a funny face
- Imitate a professional wrestler
- Trip and fall

To begin, one player from each team goes to the front of the room. In our game, Adam and Kyle go forward first. Adam starts by pulling out a slip of paper. Without showing anyone what is on the slip, he begins acting what is described on the paper. His goal is to get the person from the opposing team—Kyle—to smile or laugh in less than 10 seconds! If the other player keeps a straight face the entire 10 seconds, his team receives a point. If the actor makes the other player smile, the actor's team receives a point. Start another round by having a new person from each team come to the front. The process repeats so that everyone has a chance to both act and be the person trying not to smile. The first team to score 15 points is the winner!

WHEEL OF GUESSING

 # OF PLAYERS: 4 or more

PLAYERS: John, Megan, Anna, Steven

OBJECTS NEEDED: Papers, Pencils, Poster Board (or dry erase board)

OR MORE

....

Much like the popular game show, *Wheel of Fortune®,* teams compete to be the first to discover phrases. You'll need a dry erase board, a large poster board, or slips of paper to write down letters of the alphabet. Divide players into two teams. Each player should write a short phrase (3 - 6 words long) on a small slip of paper. The phrases can be from any random category. Players keep their own written phrases to themselves and do not show them to anyone (including their teammates).

A player from Team A goes first—in our game it is Megan. She draws a space for each letter in each word of her phrase—like playing *Hangman.* (The person who wrote the phrase does not guess or participate with her team for that round; instead she writes the letters on the board as the teams make guesses.) Team B guesses first—either a consonant or a vowel. If that letter is anywhere in the phrase, Megan fills in the appropriate spaces and that team gets to guess again. If the letter is not present in the phrase, the next team guesses.

Play continues until one team guesses the phrase correctly. Teams are limited to three guesses per round—if a team guesses correctly after three incorrect guesses, they do not earn a point. The team that does guess the phrase correctly in three or less guesses receives one point. Rounds continue with different players going to the front until one team has scored five points to win the game!

WHO ARE YOU?

 # OF PLAYERS: 6 or more
PLAYERS: Everyone!
OBJECTS NEEDED: Nothing

This game isn't extremely competitive but it certainly keeps everyone laughing! Divide players into two teams and have everyone sit in a circle. The *hot spot* is a chair in the middle of the circle. Team A starts by sending a teammate to sit in the *hot spot*—she must keep her eyes closed for the entire round (no peaking). After Team A's player has closed her eyes, Team B sends a teammate to interact with the player in the center. Team B's player must disguise his voice so that the person in the *hot spot* won't discover his identity.

The person in the *hot spot* asks random questions to her opponent—in this case Rachel is in the *hot spot* and Kyle is disguising his voice. The questions and answers are irrelevant—the only thing that is important is for Kyle to protect his identity. After Rachel asks the first question—and the reply is in a funny, weird, disguised voice—she guesses who she thinks the person is who is disguising his voice. If she guesses correctly on the first try, her team receives five points. If she guesses wrong, she must ask a second question—and Kyle will give another random, disguised answer. If she then guesses correctly, her team receives three points. If she guesses correctly after a third question, her team only receives one point. If Rachel does not guess correctly after three guesses, Kyle's team gets five points. Play continues with one of Team B's players in the *hot spot* and someone from Team A disguising her voice until everyone has taken a turn in the *hot spot*. The first team to reach 30 points wins!

WHO'S THE SMARTEST?

 # OF PLAYERS: 6 or more
PLAYERS: Anna, Megan, Rachel, Kyle, Adam, Steven
OBJECTS NEEDED: Paper, Pencils, Bowl

Some intelligence and speed are required for this extremely fun game! Each player writes random fact-based questions and the correct answers on 5-7 small strips of paper. Questions can be anything factual and objective—they can range from trivia to questions about history, science, geography, pop culture, sports, foods, TV, actors, movies, etc. The game works best when questions are based on general knowledge that everyone should know. As players are writing questions, they should strive to make them difficult enough to challenge their opponents, but not so hard that their own teammates won't know the answers. Players keep their questions—they do not show them to anyone, not even their teammates. Divide players into two teams.

Team A begins by sending one player to the front to read one of her questions to the entire group. After the player reads the question, each team collaborates quietly to determine the team's answer. After roughly 30 seconds of discussion, teams write their answer on a piece of paper. Teams then simultaneously show their answers to the player who asked the question. If a team answered the question correctly, it receives a point. It is possible for both teams to receive a point. If no team answers the question correctly, neither team receives a point. (The player reading the question cannot help or participate with the answer to that question). Play continues with the other team sending a player to read a question to the group. This process repeats so that every player gets a chance to ask her questions. The first team to score 20 points is the winner!

WILD EIGHTS

 # OF PLAYERS: 2 or more
PLAYERS: Adam, Rachel, Sarah, John
OBJECTS NEEDED: Deck of Cards

OR MORE

Begin by explaining the card rules listed below and dealing eight cards to each player. The remaining cards are placed face down in the center with one card flipped face up to form a discard pile. The player to the dealer's left starts by playing a card that either matches the suit or the number of the center face up card. The next player then plays a card that matches the suit or number of the card just played. If a player cannot play the proper card, he must pick up a card from the center pile for his turn. Play continues around the circle. The goal is to be the player who plays all his cards first! The person who gets rid of his cards the fastest receives one point. Reshuffle, deal again, and the first player to reach three points wins the game!

Wild Eights card rules:

- 2s reverse play
- 5s skip the next player
- 10s require the player to the left to draw one card
- 8s are wild (they can be used as anything)

21

 # OF PLAYERS: 4 or more
PLAYERS: Kyle, Megan, Anna, Steven
OBJECTS NEEDED: Deck of Cards, Jelly Beans (or some other candy)

OR MORE

Each player starts with seven jelly beans. The goal is to keep yours and try to win everyone else's jelly beans! To begin every round, each person *antes* by putting one of her jelly beans into the middle. One card is dealt face down to each player, followed by one card dealt face up to each player. Players can see all the face up cards, but each player peeks at her face down card to keep everyone else from seeing the card. The goal is to add the value of each card and be the closest to 21 points.

Card values in *21* are as follows:

- Aces = 1 or 11 points
- Face cards = 10 points
- All other cards = face value
- An Ace and a black Jack (either one) beats any other combination

After all the players have looked at both of their cards, the person to the left of the dealer says either *hit* or *stop*. *Hit* simply means that player wants another card, and the dealer gives him one more card face down (a player would do this if the value of his two cards was low enough that another card might get him closer to 21). Saying *stop* means that player has 21 points or is close to it and he does not want another card. If, however, a player says *hit* and he receives a card that puts him over 21 points, he is out for that round. When a player says *hit,* after looking at the new card, he can up his *ante* as much as he wants. This continues until everyone has stopped hitting and the *ante* is fixed. At this point, everyone who is still playing reveals all cards, and the person closest to 21 wins the *ante* of jelly beans. Another round begins with everyone placing another *ante* and dealing cards. Play repeats until one player wins all the jelly beans, or whoever has the most after a designated time.

VARIATION: Another option is that the person who wins each round can set a new point value—instead of trying to get 21, players try to get 24 or 17, or even 40, etc.

99

 # OF PLAYERS: 3 or more
PLAYERS: Adam, Rachel, Kyle, Megan
OBJECTS NEEDED: Deck of Cards, Pennies

OR MORE

Each player starts the game with five pennies. To begin, deal three cards to each player. The remainder of the deck is placed face down in the middle as a draw pile. Players can look at their cards. Card values are as follows:

- Aces = 1 or 11 (points)
- Kings = 50
- Queens & Jacks = 10
- 10s = plus or minus 10 (player can choose)

- 9s = skip a player (and also worth 9 points)
- 4s = reverse directions (and also worth 4 points)
- All others = face value

Adam begins by playing any one of his three cards to form a discard pile. After each turn, players take a card from the middle pile so each player always has three cards. Next, Rachel plays any one of her three cards and takes another card. As each card is played, the point values are added together. If Adam played a 4 and Rachel played a 7, there are 11 points on the pile. Play continues around the circle until the value of the discard pile reaches or exceeds 99 points! The player whose card made the value of the pile 99 or higher loses one of his pennies. When that happens, flip the discard pile over, place it under the middle pile, start tallying cards at zero and resume play. The game continues until only one person has any pennies left.

FAMILY & GROUP GAMES
·········· OUTDOORS ··········

AROUND THE WORLD

 # OF PLAYERS: 2 or more
PLAYERS: Adam, Megan, Steven, Anna, Rachel
OBJECTS NEEDED: Basketball, Basketball Hoop

OR MORE

To begin, designate 10 spots around the key of a basketball court. One spot, for example, might be at the free-throw line, another at the 3-point line, a few around the key, a lay-up type shot, etc. The goal is to be the first player to make a shot from each of the 10 spots. Adam starts at Spot #1. If he makes his shot from that spot, he advances to Spot #2. If he makes his shot from the Spot #2, he advances to Spot #3, etc. around the court—or *around the world!*

Once Adam misses a shot, his turn ends and it is the next player's turn. Megan also starts at Spot #1 and shoots to try to advance around the court in order from spot to spot. Eventually, each player takes a turn. When it is time for Adam's second turn, he begins shooting at the spot where he last missed. Throughout the game, each player also gets three *bonus* shots. If a player misses a shot, he may choose to use one of his *bonus* shots—if he makes the shot, he moves on. This process repeats and the first player to make all 10 shots receives a point. Play continues with more rounds. The first player to score three points wins!

BALLOON POPPING ANARCHY

 # OF PLAYERS: 6 or more
PLAYERS: Everyone!
OBJECTS NEEDED: Balloons, String (yarn, ribbon, etc.)

OR MORE

This game can be played in a gym or outside. Each player blows up one balloon and ties it off—inflated balloons must be at least 6 inches wide. Using a small piece of string, each player ties one end to the balloon and the other end around his/her ankle. Players choose whether to have a lot of slack with the string, or to tie the balloon close to their ankles. There are no teams—the goal is to try to pop everyone else's balloon without letting anyone pop yours!

RULES

- Players cannot push, shove, hold, pull, or do anything physical while trying to pop an opponent's balloon.
- Players must keep their hands behind their backs at all times— no hands are allowed to help a player maneuver in this game.
- Players cannot hide in a corner and hide their balloon—they must be actively pursuing others in the playing area.

The only way to pop another player's balloon is to simply step on it with your feet and pop it. Once a player's balloon has been popped, that person is out for that round and must sit on the side until the next round. The player who is the last person with an inflated balloon is the winner and receives a point. Start a new round with everyone receiving another ballon. The first player to score three points wins.

VARIATION: Team play. Divide players into teams of 2 - 3. The team with all their players (or even one of the teammates) remaining at the end earns a point. The first team to three points wins.

BALLOON SOCCER WAR

 # OF PLAYERS: 4 or more
PLAYERS: Everyone!
OBJECTS NEEDED: 4 large cardboard boxes, Bag of balloons, Timer

OR MORE

This game can be played in a gym or outside. In preparation, blow up lots of balloons. Designate a 20 x 20 yard area for playing the game. Place a large, open cardboard box in each of the four corners—these boxes are the team *goals*. Place approximately 30 balloons in the center of the area and divide players into four equal teams. Each team begins by standing in its respective corner.

The objective for each team is to get as many balloons as possible into the opponent's *goals,* while protecting their own *goal* by not letting other teams score. At "Go," each team races to the middle to start kicking balloons toward their opponent's *goals*—any opponent will do! Players can only use their feet, legs, shoulders and head—using hands and arms is *not* allowed in this game. Once a player advances a balloon near an opponent's *goal,* she must kick the balloon into the air and try (without using her arms or hands) to get the balloon inside the opponent's *goal*. The opponent may also be trying to prevent the same balloon from going into the box. Thus, there can be no pushing, holding or laying across the *goal* to prevent a balloon from entering. Once a balloon falls into a *goal* (box), teams cannot remove the balloons.

As balloons are used to score goals, an independent person who is not playing adds more balloons to the center area. Each round lasts five minutes. At the end of each round, the team with the fewest balloons in its goal receives a point. Play continues and the team that scores three points first is the winner!

VARIATION: Play with only two teams and two *goals*. This version is simply *balloon soccer*; but, rather than playing with one ball, there will be 30 balls (balloons). The team that scores the most at the end of each round receives a point. The first team to score three points wins!

BASE-KETBALL

OR MORE

 # OF PLAYERS: 6 or more
PLAYERS: Everyone!
OBJECTS NEEDED: Nerf® or Wiffle Bat & Ball, Basketball Hoop

Divide players into two teams. The game is played on an outside basketball hoop or in a gym with at least one basketball hoop. Begin by setting up a normal baseball diamond with three bases and a home plate—each base should be roughly 25' to 30' apart. Team A is up to *bat* first, while Team B begins in the outfield. Like normal baseball, one player from Team A stands at home base with the bat, and Team B pitches (throws a ball). Team A's player tries to hit the ball (players on each team take turns batting and pitching each inning). A swing without hitting the ball is a strike. Three strikes equal an out in this game, but there are five outs per inning. If a player hits the ball into the air and the fielding team catches it, that play counts as an out. When a player hits a line drive, or the fielding team does not catch it, then the game gets interesting—the basketball hoop comes into play!

When this happens, the outfield team must throw the ball to the end of the gym and make a shot in the basketball hoop with the ball. Once a player touches the ball, he cannot run or move with the ball—he can only throw it or advance it to a teammate. The player who hit the ball keeps running around the bases until the basketball shot is made by the opposing team. When the ball goes through the hoop, the player running the bases must stop exactly where he is. Unlike normal baseball, players do not need to be standing on a base to be safe—a player running midway between bases stops where he is when the ball goes through the hoop. Runners must touch each base before reaching home plate in order to score a point.

In this game, the fielding team does not tag bases or tag runners like in normal baseball, they simply want to advance the ball and get it through the hoop as quickly as possible. The next player on Team A goes to bat, and play continues until Team A gets five outs. At that point, Team B's players go to bat and Team A's go to the outfield. The team that scores the most points after five innings is the winner!

BASKETBALL DUEL

 # OF PLAYERS: 2 or more

PLAYERS: Anna, Sarah

OBJECTS NEEDED: 2 Basketballs, Basketball Hoop

OR MORE

The object is to be the player with the most points at the end of three rounds. For the first round, Anna tries to make as many baskets as she can by shooting 10 shots from any one spot around the 3-point line. Sarah does the same—she attempts 10 shots from any one spot around the 3-point line. Each player keeps a tally of how many shots she made during each round. For the second round, players take turns shooting 10 shots from the free throw line. For the final round, players designate any 10 shots around the key and each takes a turn shooting. The player with the most shots made at the end of the three rounds is the winner!

VARIATION: Rather than playing this fun game one-on-one, play on teams of 2-3 players. Thus, whichever team makes the most at the end of the three rounds is the winner. Also, add a twist by timing the play—each player gets one minute to make as many shots as possible. After each teammate takes a turn for each round, the team with the most points wins!

VARIATION: A classic basketball duel is a game called *H.O.R.S.E.* (the shorter version is *P.I.G.*). Anna starts by shooting the ball from anywhere she wants on the court. If she misses, Sarah can shoot from wherever she chooses. If, however, Anna makes her shot, then Sarah must shoot from that exact spot. If Sarah does make the shot, then Anna chooses a new place to make a shot. If Sarah misses, she gets an *H* and Anna chooses a new shot. Play continues with players trying to avoid missing shots so they won't spell *H.O.R.S.E.* The player still in once everyone else spells *H.O.R.S.E.* is the winner!

BASKET-DODGE BALL RACE

 # OF PLAYERS: 8 or more

PLAYERS: Everyone!

OR MORE

OBJECTS NEEDED: 4 Basketballs, A Gym with 2 Basketball Hoops, A Soft Nerf® Ball

Divide players into four even teams, and get ready for a fun basketball-dodgeball competition! Each team needs a basketball. Each team should line up in its own corner of the basketball court. To keep things fair, the line should be in order of age and skill level—a child could be the first in line from each team, then a more skilled player, etc. Place the soft Nerf® ball at center court.

At "Go," the first player from each team takes his team's basketball and runs to the other end of the court. Once he gets to the free throw line, each player tries to make a free throw shot—two players shooting at each hoop. Players must shoot every shot from the free throw line. When shots are missed, players must rebound the ball and go back to the free throw line to shoot until they make it from there (to help young players, allow them to make lay-up shots). When a shot is made, the team receives one point and the player runs back to his team's corner.

However, these four players shooting at the same time are also in a race—a race to be the first player to make a shot and get safely back to the team's corner. The first of the four to make a shot gets to run to mid-court, pick up the Nerf® ball and throw it at the remaining three players that are still shooting. If this player hits one of the three shooters, that shooter immediately returns to her team's corner. If one of the three other shooters makes a shot and is running toward her team corner, that person isn't safe until she tags the team's corner. If a shooter is hit with the ball (while shooting or while running back), her team point is taken away. If a player makes his shot and returns safely to his team corner, the team gets to keep the point.

Note that the person throwing can only throw the Nerf® ball from the center mid-court circle. Thus, after every throw, he must retrieve the ball, run back to center court, and attempt another throw. Once all of the three other shooters have either made their shots and returned safely, or been hit by the thrower, the thrower stops and that leg of the relay is over. The next leg begins with each team sending the next player in line to begin shooting. Play repeats until all players from each team have had a turn shooting (with fewer players, each teammate may need to go more than once). The team with the most points after each player has taken a turn wins!

BLINDFOLDED TEAM CHALLENGE

 # OF PLAYERS: 8 or more
PLAYERS: Everyone!
OBJECTS NEEDED: 4 Blindfolds, Random Objects
(trash can, ball, shoe, pillow, blanket, sweater, stick, broom, chair, etc.)

OR MORE

In preparation, set up the course by marking two *end lines* about 30' apart and two sideline boundaries roughly 30' wide (thus forming a large square). Inside the square, place approximately 20 random objects on the ground. These objects can be anything—trashcans, tables, balls, shoes, coats, blankets, brooms, chairs, etc. The objects should be randomly scattered throughout the playing area between the *end lines*. Divide players into two equal teams—Team A starts at one *end line* and Team B starts on the opposite *end line*.

To begin, two players from each team are blindfolded. At "Go," the two players from each team must quickly (and carefully) cross the course to the opposite *end line* (there will be four players on the course). As players maneuver through the course, they cannot touch an obstacle, run into or touch a teammate, run into an opponent, or go out of bounds. If one of these things happens, that player must return to the *end line* and start again (if two players run into each other, both must go back).

The teams at the respective *end lines* yell to guide their blindfolded teammates through the course. Since there are four players maneuvering at a time and half the players are moving in opposite directions, this can be quite challenging! Once a player reaches the opposite *end line,* he takes off the blindfold, runs back to his team and gives a teammate the blindfold. The new teammate must proceed through the course blindfolded as well. The first team to get every teammate safely across the course wins!

BOCCE

 # OF PLAYERS: 2 or more
PLAYERS: Anna, Rachel
OBJECTS NEEDED: Many Balls

OR MORE

This popular version of lawn bowling requires a steady arm, good aim, and some strategy. One ball is chosen to be the *main* ball—the ball that each player tries to hit each round. Each player needs her own ball (balls should be round or circular, not too big, and the heavier the better). Play begins by throwing the *main* ball into the playing field, roughly 30' away. Each player, in turn, takes her own ball and tries to roll it as close as possible to the *main* ball.

It is possible to knock another player's ball out of the way to get your ball closer—in fact, it is a smart strategy! After each player has rolled her ball, the player whose ball is closest to the *main* ball receives three points. The player's ball that is next closest receives one point. If a player's ball is both the closest and touches the main ball—she earns five points. The player whose ball was the closest picks up the *main* ball and throws it again about 30' away (in any direction, wherever she wants). Players again take turns trying to get the closet to the *main* ball. The first person to score 30 points is the winner!

BOTTOM BALL

 # OF PLAYERS: 4 or more
PLAYERS: Adam, John, Steven, Kyle
OBJECTS NEEDED: Balloons, 4 Chairs, Yarn

OR MORE

In preparation, place two chairs about 20' apart. Using a long piece of string (or yarn), tie one end to the top of one chair and the other end to the top of the other chair. Since the string is the *net* for the game, it needs to be tight and about 3' from the ground. Place the other two chairs perpendicular to the first two, also 20' apart, and tie a string between those two chairs as well. The two strings should intersect midway, forming four equal sections between the chairs. Divide players into pairs—four pairs begin the game by having one pair sit in each of the four sections. Each player sits and remains on his bottom throughout the game.

At "Go," throw about six balloons into the middle of the playing area (between the four chairs, into any section). Each pair's goal is to prevent a balloon from falling into their section and hitting the ground. Players protect their sections by preventing balloons from hitting the ground, and try to offensively hit balloons and make them land in another pair's section. In this game, points are not good—points are scored when a player's bottom leaves the ground or a balloon lands in his section. It may be necessary to have an independent judge (perhaps for each pair) watch and tally points for each pair. These four pairs play for three minutes, and the pair that has the least amount of points at the end of the round (three minutes) receives a point. This is a good point! If there are other pairs, they rotate in replacing the losing pairs. The first pair to win five rounds is the winner!

VARIATION: With fewer players, have one person sit in each section.

VARIATION: Use a single string (or one *net*). Play volleyball with teams of three. Players must remain on their bottoms, and they only have three hits to get the balloon over to the opponent's side.

BOWLING DODGE BALL

 # OF PLAYERS: 6 or more

PLAYERS: Everyone!

OBJECTS NEEDED: About 10-15 Balls (basketballs, footballs, volleyballs, Nerf® balls, tennis balls, soccer balls, etc), 10 Plastic Cups or Bottles.

OR MORE

This game is played in a gym. Place five plastic cups or bottles on each end of the gym—line them up horizontally about 7' apart near the wall or baseline. Divide players into two equal teams. Each team starts on its own side and has half of the random balls. The goal is to be the first team to knock over the other team's five cups *(pins)*.

At "Go," teams can roll, throw or even kick the balls to the opposite side, and the balls keep going back and forth. If a player is hit with a ball in this game, it does not matter—teams are simply trying to knock over the opponent's *pins* while protecting their own team's *pins*. As the balls come over to a team's side, players can knock down or stop the ball any way they want to prevent the ball from hitting the team's *pins*. The team that first knocks over their opponent's five *pins* receives a point. Start another round and the first team to score three points is the winner!

RULES

- Players cannot purposely try to hit opponents with a ball.
- Teams cannot go onto the other team's side (designate a *middle line* that players cannot cross).
- On each side, there is a 5' section in front of the *pins* that no player can enter (players can only enter this section to retrieve a ball—they cannot block balls while in this section).

CAPTURE THE FLAG

 # OF PLAYERS: 8 or more
PLAYERS: Everyone!
OBJECTS NEEDED: 2 Old Shirts

OR MORE

This classic night game is played in a large field or park but can also be played in neighborhoods between streets and homes. In preparation, set up the field by establishing a *middle line* that clearly separates each team's side. There are no other boundaries, but players must know where the *middle line* is at all times. Each team takes a *flag* (an old shirt) and places it in a designated area about 50 yards away from the middle line. For the first round, teams know where each other's *flags* are located. As rounds progress, play becomes more difficult as each team hides its *flag*. Each team needs to establish a *jail* area—a 10' x 10' area roughly 30 yards from the middle line. Divide players into two equal teams— each teams starts on its respective side.

The purpose of the game is to capture the opposing team's *flag* and bring it back without being caught. Teams should develop two strategies: how to capture the opponent's *flag* and how to protect their own *flag*. Players can choose to run openly to the opposing side or try to sneak across covertly. Since it is dark and there are no side boundaries, players have ample space to cross—that's why the *middle line* must be known by all. As players move away from the center of play, there should be no confusion about the placement of the *middle line*.

If a player crosses the *middle line* into the opposing team's side and is tagged by an opponent, she is sent to *jail*. A player can be released from *jail* by having one of her teammates tag her while she's in *jail*. Only one player can be freed at a time—and if she's tagged on the way back to her side, she still must go back to *jail* (there are no free walk backs). After a player is released from *jail*, she cannot immediately capture the opponent's *flag*— she must return to her own side first (this rule also applies to the teammate who released her from *jail*).

If a player captures the *flag* and then is tagged on the way back to his side, he not only goes to *jail*, the *flag* goes back to its original position. The only other rule is that teams cannot closely guard their *flag*. There should be at least a 10' radius around each team's *flag* that the guarding team cannot enter (this prevents teams from staying right next to the *flag* to make it impossible to capture). The winning team is the one that captures the opponent's *flag* and brings it safely to their own team's side first!

VARIATION: Each team has four *flags*. These *flags* are placed about 50 yards from the *middle line* in a horizontal row side by side about 30' apart. The rules are the same—except a player can only grab one flag at a time. The first team that successfully captures and brings all four of their opponent's *flags* to their side is the winner!

CONCEALED MOVEMENT

 # OF PLAYERS: 4 or more
PLAYERS: Adam, Steven, Anna, Megan
OBJECTS NEEDED: Flashlight

OR MORE

There are no teams in this game. One person starts by being *it*—in our game it is Adam—and he has a flashlight. *It* counts to 100 while the remaining players go and hide. After counting, *it* tries to find the other players who are hiding (although similar to *Hide & Go Seek*, in this game *it* must find and shine the light on the hiding players). The goal of course is to be the last person found by *it*.

The twist to this fun game is that those hiding do not have to stay in one place—they can move around as long as they are not spotted by *it* with the flashlight. For example, if Adam walks past Steven and doesn't spot him in his hiding place—Steven can (but does not have to) move to a different spot as often as he likes to avoid being found. When Adam does spot a player and shines the light on her, she is out and must sit on the sidelines until the next round. The last person found receives three points. Play repeats so that everyone has a chance to be *it*. The first player to score 10 points is the winner!

VARIATION: Play as pairs! Two teammates must hide together. The duo that is *it* has two people looking with a flashlight. The last pair found receives three points!

DELICATE BALLOON OBSTACLE COURSE

 # OF PLAYERS: 6 or more
PLAYERS: Everyone!
OBJECTS NEEDED: 2 Cookie Sheets, Balloons, Random Objects
(chairs, tables, garbage cans, etc.)

OR MORE

Begin by establishing a starting line and middle line about 40' apart. Between these two lines, place about 10 objects (or barriers) randomly throughout the course. Examples of barriers include chairs, tables, garbage cans, etc. Everyone collaborates to decide which objects players will go over, under, around, etc.— each player must go through the course the same way. Divide players into two equal teams. Each team needs one cookie sheet and each player needs a balloon (balloons should not be blown up yet).

At "Go," one player from each team takes her own balloon, blows it up, ties it off and places the inflated balloon on the team's cookie sheet. She must then run the obstacle course, going around, over and under the barriers in the pre-established pattern to the middle line and back. Players are trying to ensure that the balloon does not fall off the cookie sheet as they run. If the balloon does fall off, that player must pick up the balloon and put it back on the cookie sheet before she can start running forward again.

Players also cannot touch or hold the balloon with any part of their bodies while running—except to pick it up when it falls. Once a player makes it to the middle line and back, she hands the cookie sheet to the next player on her team. The next player takes his own balloon, blows it up and ties it off, and runs the course with the balloon on the cookie sheet. The team whose players complete the course the quickest is the winner!

DODGEBALL CAPTURE THE FLAG

 # OF PLAYERS: 10 or more
PLAYERS: Everyone!
OBJECTS NEEDED: 2 towels, 10+ balls

OR MORE

This combination of two classic games is certain to be a hit with everyone! Divide players into two equal teams, and separate the gym area into equal sides for each team. On both sides, take a towel (the *flag)* and place it in the middle of the back wall on the floor. Each team starts on its own side with an equal amount of balls. The balls can be anything—volleyballs, footballs, soccer balls, basketballs, or ideally some Nerf® or softer balls.

Teams can win the game in two different ways. First, if a team throws balls and hits every player on the opposing team to get them out. Second, a player from one team captures the other team's *flag* and makes it back to his team's side without being hit by a ball from the opposing team.

At "Go," teams begin throwing balls back and forth trying to hit the opposing team's players. When a ball hits a player, that player must go to the opposing team's *jail—jails* are simply a 5' x 5' corner of the gym for each team. If, however, a player catches a ball, then that player is safe and does not have to go to *jail* (the player who threw the ball does not have to go to *jail* either). Teammates can rescue other teammates from *jail* by running across the opposing side and touching just one person in *jail,* which sets everyone in *jail* free. The freed players all get to go back to their side safely without being hit as they return. If a person is hit on his way to free teammates from *jail,* or trying to capture the *flag,* that person must go to *jail.* Any player freed from *jail* cannot leave the jail and immediately go get the flag—he must return to his side first.

If a player captures the *flag* and is hit by a ball as she returns to her side, that person goes to *jail* and the *flag* is returned to its original spot. The first team to capture their opponent's *flag* and bring it safely to their side, or, hit every other player on the opposing team with a ball, receives a point. Start another round, and the team that wins three rounds first is the winner!

FEET-BALL

 # OF PLAYERS: 6 or more
PLAYERS: Megan, Steven, John, Sarah, Anna, Rachel
OBJECTS NEEDED: 2 Chairs, String, Balloons

OR MORE

Playing volleyball with your feet may sound strange, but it's a lot of fun! Place two chairs about 12' apart and tie a string between the tops of the two chairs. The string should be roughly 3' off the ground since it is the *net* for the game. Divide players into teams of three and blow up a balloon to use as the ball (have extra balloons handy in case some pop).

The object of the game is to play volleyball—but players hit the "ball" with their feet, not their hands. Two teams compete at a time, but since games go quickly other teams can easily rotate into play. Team A starts on one side of the *net* and Team B starts on the other. All players must sit (or lie) on the ground. To begin, Team A throws the balloon over the *net* onto Team B's side. Team B has three hits to get the balloon back over the *net* onto Team A's side. Players can only use their feet to hit the balloon—no hands, arms, heads, etc.—and no standing is allowed during any part of the competition! Also, the same player can hit the balloon twice in a row, but not three times— if it takes all three hits to get the balloon over the *net*, at least two teammates must hit the balloon.

If the balloon does not make it over the *net* before the third hit, or the balloon falls on a team's side, the other team receives a point (just like in volleyball). There are no out of bounds in this game, but when the balloon crosses over the *net,* it must go between the two chairs. Once a team has scored five points, the losing team is replaced with a new team, and the team who won receives a point for winning that round. The team that wins five rounds first is the winner!

FOUR CORNER DODGEBALL

OR MORE

 # OF PLAYERS: 6 or more
PLAYERS: Steven, Megan, Adam, Rachel, Anna, John
OBJECTS NEEDED: 6 soft balls

While normal *Dodgeball* is fun, this creative version is much more exciting! A gym area and six soft balls are needed to play. Divide players into teams of three. One team starts by being the *throwers*. The *throwers* goal is to throw the balls at the *runners* to prevent them from getting points. The *runners* (everyone not on the *throwers* team), runs from corner to corner in the gym and along the walls—their goal is to earn points by successfully making it to corners without being hit by a ball.

Each corner has an imaginary 5' x 5' box around it that is a *safe zone*. If a *runner* is in the *safe zone,* he cannot be hit with a ball. A player can only stay in the *safe zone* for 10 seconds. If, however, a *runner* is running between corners and gets hit by a ball, he gets a *strike*. Once a player is hit twice, or gets his second *strike,* he must sit on the sideline until the next round starts. Each time a *runner* makes it safely to another corner without being hit, he receives a point.

The rules are as follows:
- A *thrower* cannot hit a *runner* in the head—if this happens it does not count as a strike against the *runner*.
- The *throwers* must throw from a 10' x 10' box in the middle of the gym.
- Once the *throwers* have thrown all their balls at the *runners,* they can retrieve the balls.
- When retrieving balls, the *throwers* cannot throw a ball at a *runner* until they are back in the middle box.
- To prevent *runners* from kicking or moving the balls so the *throwers* cannot get them, anytime a *runner* touches a ball, it counts as a strike (even if the *runner* mistakenly steps on a ball when running).

Throwers thus have the incentive to get all the *runners* out as soon as possible to prevent them from gaining points. At the end of each round, teams total the points earned—for example, if one teammate received three points by reaching three corners before getting two strikes and another teammate received five points, and the third teammate received six points, that team scored 14 for that round. Start another round with a new team taking their turn as the *throwers*. The first team to score 100 points is the winner!

FOX & GEESE

 # OF PLAYERS: 3 or more
PLAYERS: Adam, Rachel, Steven
OBJECTS NEEDED: Snow

OR MORE

After the next fresh snowfall, go to the backyard or park to play this chilly version of tag. Players begin by collectively stomping a large circle to compact the snow. The circle should be about 30' in diameter, but just the outer edge of the circle needs to be compacted—not the inner area. The compacted snow around the circle's edge should form a path wide enough for someone to run on (roughly a foot wide). Once the circle is created, everyone stomps random paths within the circle (also about a foot wide). Some paths can be straight lines, others can curve, and most should connect with other paths. The paths need to meet because players run from path to path in this game of tag. In the middle of the large circle create a much smaller circle, about 5' x 5' wide. The entire portion of the small circle must be compacted—this circle is *home base*.

To begin, one person is the *fox* and all the other players are *geese*. The *fox* and the *geese* run through the paths, and the *fox* tries to tag one of the *geese*. Once the *fox* tags one of the *geese*, the tagged player becomes the *fox* (like normal tag). Once a player has been the *fox* three times, he is out for that round. The player who is still in the game once everyone else is out is the winner! The rules are:

- Everyone running must stay on a path. There is no running outside the circle, or between the designated paths—if this happens, the player who stepped out of the path becomes the *fox*.

- A player is safe and cannot be tagged when she is in the *home base*. A player cannot stay in *home base* for more than 10 seconds.

FRISBEE® BASEBALL

 # OF PLAYERS: 6 or more
PLAYERS: Everyone!
OBJECTS NEEDED: Frisbee®, Garbage Can

OR MORE

All skill levels enjoy this extremely fun mixture of *Frisbee®* and *Baseball*. To begin, use a baseball diamond or set up a typical baseball field with three bases, home plate and an outfield. Place a garbage can (or bucket) at home plate. Divide players into two equal teams. Team A starts by being up to "bat," and Team B starts in the outfield. *Batting* in this game is simply throwing the Frisbee® into the outfield. The Frisbee® can be thrown wherever a player chooses as long as it lands inside the foul ball lines. Players take turns being the Frisbee® thrower. Unlike baseball, there are no outs in this game. Each team has 20 throws per inning and the goal is to score as many points as possible with those throws.

Once a thrower tosses the Frisbee®, she runs to 1st base, then to 2nd base, etc. just like in normal baseball. The goal for the fielding team is to catch or retrieve the Frisbee®, and as quickly as possible advance it toward home plate, and place it inside the garbage can (or bucket). Once the Frisbee® is in the garbage can, the player running the bases must stop. In this game, a runner does not have to be on a base to be safe, he must stop wherever he is (or go back to where he was) when the Frisbee® goes into the garbage can.

Because there are no outs, it does not matter if the fielding team catches the Frisbee® before it hits the ground, nor do they try to tag runners. Their only goal is to get the Frisbee® into the garbage can as quickly as possible. Whenever a player has the Frisbee®, she cannot run with it—once she gets the Frisbee® she must throw it from where she is. Because of this, teams may want to designate a player (catcher) to stay near the garbage can. Teammates can try to throw directly to the catcher, or strategically advance the Frisbee® from teammate to teammate until it gets into the garbage can. For example, if Adam throws the Frisbee® to Anna at the garbage can, but Anna misses it, she has to run to get the Frisbee®. Anna can't just run back and place it in the garbage can. Like the other players, she cannot move with the Frisbee®. She must throw it to another teammate so it can be placed in the garbage can.

The team at bat tries to score as many runs as possible. A run is scored just like in baseball—a player goes around all the bases and makes it back to home base. Runners must stop, even if mid-base, whenever the Frisbee® goes into the garbage can. When a runner is on a base, or mid-base, he cannot start running again toward home base until the Frisbee® (from the next teammate's throw) has touched the ground or a player from the opposing team touches it. After a team's 20 throws for the inning, the teams switch places. The team with the most points after five innings is the winner!

FRISBEE® FOOTBALL

 # OF PLAYERS: 6 or more
PLAYERS: Adam, Rachel, Steven, John, Megan, Anna
OBJECTS NEEDED: Frisbee®

OR MORE

Set up the playing field by establishing end zones about 70 yards apart and sidelines about 30-40 yards wide. Divide players into two equal teams. Like football, teams try to advance the Frisbee® down the field to score touchdowns. The game begins with one team "kicking-off," which entails throwing the Frisbee® down the field to the opposing team. The receiving team either catches or picks up the Frisbee® and will start throwing it back and forth between teammates to advance down the field.

When a player has the Frisbee®, she cannot run or move more than two steps—the goal is to throw the Frisbee® to another teammate. Players throw the Frisbee® from teammate to teammate to move it down the field. Unlike football, there are no huddles or plays—players continue to run, try to get open, catch the Frisbee®, and continue to advance it down the field. If the Frisbee® is thrown and a player drops it, it is a turnover and the other team gets to start throwing from that spot. Turnovers also occur when the defending team knocks down or intercepts the Frisbee®. When a turnover happens, play starts where the Frisbee® was dropped or intercepted. The other team now tries to move the Frisbee® in the opposite direction toward their end zone. Each time a team advances the Frisbee® into their end zone, they receive one point. The scoring team "kicks off" and play repeats. The team that scores 10 points first is the winner!

Other rules include:
- Opposing players can guard the player throwing, but everyone must give throwers at least a 3' radius.
- Once a player catches the Frisbee®, he cannot run or advance more than two steps.
- If the Frisbee® or a player goes out of bounds, it is a turnover.
- Players cannot hold, grab or push off each other at any time.

FRISBEE® GOLF

 # OF PLAYERS: 2 or more
PLAYERS: Anna, Rachel
OBJECTS NEEDED: Frisbee® for Each Player (or plastic lids)

OR MORE

Begin by setting up a nine-hole *golf course* using random objects outside as the *holes*. Examples of *holes* include trees, fence posts, bushes, rocks, shoes, poles, etc. Each player needs a Frisbee® or disk of some kind. Players throw their Frisbees® from hole to hole, trying to hit each *hole* in as few throws as possible (just like playing golf). If, for example, it takes Anna three throws to hit *hole #1* and Rachel makes it in four throws, each player receives a point for the number of throws it took to hit the *hole*. Like golf, the player with the lowest score (least amount of points/throws) at the end of the nine *holes* is the winner!

GROUP SARDINES

 # OF PLAYERS: 6 or more
PLAYERS: Everyone!
OBJECTS NEEDED: Timer

OR MORE

This classic game is the opposite of *Hide & Go Seek*—rather than everyone hiding, one player hides and everyone tries to find that player. This game is played in the dark, but with a twist that makes it competitive! Divide players into teams of three. One person from each team goes and hides, while all the other players stay together and wait for about three minutes to give their teammates time to find a good place. No looking is permitted while the players hide. The first and most important rule is that there is absolutely no talking allowed in this game.

The goal is to be the first team to reunite. After three minutes, another player from each team leaves the group to go seek the hidden teammate (only one person from each team leaves at one time). Every three minutes, another player from each team leaves to go seek—this continues until every player has left.

As players search, they may come across others who are hiding—if it is a player(s) from another team, they just keep searching for their own teammates. There is absolutely no talking allowed—not even to ask who someone is when he's found. If someone is caught talking, the entire team is disqualified for that round to prevent cheating. When a player finds a teammate hiding, they hide together and wait until other teammates find them. Once every player from a team has been reunited in hiding, that team stands up and yells, "We won!" That team receives a point and another round starts. The first team to score three points wins!

Important rules:

- Once a player locates a teammate(s), she must stop and hide with them.
- If two searching teammates cross paths, they cannot stay together.
- If a player from another team finds two teammates sticking together, or talking, that team is disqualified.

HASTY TUNNEL CRAWL

 # OF PLAYERS: 6 or more
PLAYERS: Everyone!
OBJECTS NEEDED: Nothing

The abnormality of this race is what makes it so fun! Begin by marking a starting line and a finishing line parallel to each other about 30' apart. Divide players into two equal teams. Each team lines up single file behind the starting line, and the goal is to get the entire team to the finish line the quickest. However, the way to get to the finish line is why this game is so unusual—and entertaining!

At "Go," the first player from each team takes one step past the starting line and spreads his legs—he doesn't want to step out too far since the next teammate in line must be able to reach out and touch him (if the player behind can't reach out and touch the player ahead, it doesn't count). Once the first person has stepped, spread his legs, and the next person behind has reached to prove that he can reach him, then the next person crawls between the legs of the first person. Once he crawls through, he stands an arm's length in front of that player. The first person reaches out to touch the player in front of him to prove they are the right distance apart and yells, "Go." The 3rd player crawls through both players spread legs and stands in front of them. This process repeats until everyone on the team has crawled to the front.

Once everyone has gone and the very first player is at the back of the line, the original first player crawls through the entire tunnel all the way to the front to begin the process again. This continues until every teammate crosses the finish line—*not* the first player across the finish line, the team that wins is the first to get *every teammate* across the finish line the fastest!

HULA HOOP BASEBALL

 # OF PLAYERS: 10 or more
PLAYERS: Everyone!
OBJECTS NEEDED: Hula Hoop, 4 Shoes (for bases)

Play this fun variation of baseball on a normal baseball diamond, or simply set up a baseball field using shoes for the bases (each base should be about 30' apart). In the middle of each of the four bases, where the pitcher's mound would normally be, designate a 5' x 5' area where players stand to throw the hula hoop. Divide players into two teams—one team starts in the outfield and the other team is up to "bat."

So players won't be hit by a flying hula hoop, everyone on the "batting" team should stand roughly 10'-20' outside the bases. Unlike baseball, there are no foul lines or a home run fence—play can encompass 360 degrees and extends as far as possible. The first "batter" will go to the throwing area (pitcher's mound), grab the hula hoop by the hand, spin around 2 - 3 times like a discus thrower, and then let the hula hoop fly! The hula hoop flies through the air in any random direction (forward, backward or sideways). Once he releases the hula hoop, the player who threw it will run around the bases starting at 1st base, then to 2nd base, then to 3rd base, then to the 4th, and finally back to the designated throwing area in the middle where he originally "batted" (home base). Once a player gets around all the bases and back to the throwing spot/home base, he earns a point for his team.

There are no outs in this game; however, if the fielding team catches the hula hoop before it hits the ground, that batter's turn is over and he does not run the bases. Play continues with the next batter throwing the hula hoop. If the hula hoop is not caught by the fielding team, or it is a line drive, the fielding team must retrieve the hula hoop and advance it to the middle 5' x 5' throwing area as quickly as possible. Once the hula hoop reaches the middle throwing area, the runner must stop running wherever he is (even if he is between bases). Since players who are running are not tagged in this game, they simply run until the hula hoop is returned to the middle section.

Once a person on the fielding team retrieves the thrown hula hoop, she cannot run with the hula hoop—she can only advance it by throwing it to another teammate. The hula hoop must go from teammate to teammate until it reaches the middle section. If a running player is between bases, she can advance when the next batter throws the hula hoop. Play continues until every teammate on the batting team has thrown the hula hoop twice, or each team has thrown 20 times for that inning. Teams switch places so the fielding team takes a turn at "bat." The batting team receives one point for every player that makes it all the way around the bases and back home. After five innings, the team with the most points wins!

HUMAN BOWLING

 # OF PLAYERS: 6 or more
PLAYERS: Everyone!
OBJECTS NEEDED: Ball

OR MORE

Divide players into two equal teams. Whether this game is played in a gym or outside, the playing area needs to be roughly 20 x 20 yards. Split that area in half, and have a team stand on each side. Team A starts as the *pins,* and Team B begins as the *bowlers.* All of the players on the *pins* team spread randomly throughout their playing area and do different random stances. Examples of stances include feet close together, on one foot, legs spread apart, sitting, etc. Once a player chooses his stance, he must remain in that same stance for the entire round or until he is out. Moving around is not allowed.

Team B's *bowlers* stand along the far line on their side of the playing area. Their goal is to try to hit each person on the opposing team in as few bowls as possible. Each person on Team B takes a turn bowling—a bowl is simply rolling or bouncing the ball at an opposing player—no throwing is allowed. Every player must bowl from the same spot—the middle point along the back line. There is no moving along the line to get a better angle when bowling. If a ball does hit a player, that player is out for that round and stands on the sidelines. Team B keeps bowling until every player on Team A (the *pins)* has been hit and they keep track of how many bowls they took. Then, Team A becomes the *bowlers* and Team B lines up randomly on their side. After Team A has hit every player on Team B, the team that eliminated the other team in the least amount of bowls receives a point. Play continues until one team has scored three points to win the game!

VARIATION: Each team lines up side by side, horizontally along their own back line. Teammates should stand roughly 1' – 2' apart, and everyone stands with legs apart. Each player takes a turn bowling, trying to roll the ball to hit the leg of an opponent. When a player's leg is hit, she must stand with both legs close together. When her legs are hit again, she is out and sits on the sidelines until the next round. Thus, each player must be hit twice in order to get them out. The first team to hit every opponent twice wins!

HUMAN KNOT

 # OF PLAYERS: 6 or more
PLAYERS: Everyone!
OBJECTS NEEDED: Nothing

OR MORE

....

While this may seem impossible, it works every time and is a ton of fun! Players begin by standing closely together to form a very small circle. Each person reaches both hands into the middle of the circle and grabs two different players' hands. A player should not grab both hands of the same person—one hand should be holding one person's hand and the other hand should be holding the hand of a different player. The object of the game is for the entire group to untangle themselves and eventually form a circle with everyone's hands untangled. In the process of doing this, players CANNOT let go of each other's hands. Thus, even when someone has to crawl though someone else's arms, players must not let go—and it works every time!

VARIATION: With more than 12 players, divide everyone into two equal teams then race to see which team untangles the fastest!

HUNTERS & PRISONERS

 # OF PLAYERS: 8 or more
PLAYERS: Everyone!
OBJECTS NEEDED: 6 Old Shirts or Towels

OR MORE

Play this extremely fun game in a large field or a park—one with many trees or places to hide works best. Begin by establishing a 20' circle in the middle of the playing area as the *hunters'* base. Place three *flags* on the ground in the center of the circle (use shirts or towels for the *flags*). About 10 yards away from the hunters' base should be a 7' circle *prison* where the *hunters* place their captured *prisoners*. Divide players into two equal teams.

One team starts by being the *hunters,* and the other team begins as the *prisoners.* The *hunters* start the game by standing in their base, closing their eyes, and counting to 100. While they count, the *prisoners* take their own three *flags* and go and hide. The *prisoners' flags* must be held by different players and cannot be dropped, left behind, or hidden at any time. Thus, any three players initially have a team *flag,* but one player cannot hold more than one *flag.*

The object of the game is to be the first team to capture all six of the *flags.* The advantage for the *hunters* is that they can tag a *prisoner* with a *flag* and send him to *jail* (thus also capturing a *flag).* The advantage for the *prisoners* is that they can run around, passing *flags* from teammate to teammate while avoiding the *hunters,* and only go to *prison* if tagged when holding a *flag.* When the game begins, the *hunters* must protect their base (with *flags* in it), go try to capture the *prisoners' flags* and send them to prison, and guard their prison once *prisoners* are in it. If one of the *prisoners' flags* is dropped, hidden, or touches the ground for any reason, the *flag* is lost and is turned over to the *hunters.* The *hunters* place the captured *flag* in the center of their base, place the tagged person in *jail* (unless the *flag* was just dropped), and then go try to capture the rest of the *prisoners' flags.* The *prisoners* not only avoid being caught by the *hunters* and protect and pass their *flags,* they also try to capture the *flags* from the *hunters'* base.

The rules for the *prisoners* are as follows:

- Only one *prisoner* is allowed in the *hunters'* base at one time.
- Only one *flag* can be taken from the *hunters'* base at one time.
- A *prisoner* is safe in the circle because the *hunters* cannot enter their own base.
- A *prisoner* can only stay in the *hunters'* base for 10 seconds, and once he leaves the base, he can be tagged immediately by a *hunter*.
- If a *prisoner* is tagged when he has a *flag,* he is sent to *jail.*
- A *prisoner* in *jail* can be freed if another teammate tags them while in *jail.*
- Only one *prisoner* can be freed at a time, but once he is freed, he can be tagged immediately.

Play continues back and forth until one team captures all six of the *flags.* The first team to do so scores one point. Teams then reverse roles so that the *prisoners* become the *hunters.* The first team to score three points wins!

ILLUMINATED PILLOWCASE FOOTBALL

 # OF PLAYERS: 6 or more
PLAYERS: Adam, Rachel, Anna, Steven, Megan, John
OBJECTS NEEDED: White Pillowcase for each Player, Glow-stick (or tennis ball)

OR MORE

This night version of Frisbee® football is a little more challenging—and a lot more fun! Begin by dividing players into two equal teams. Each player needs a white pillowcase. Set up the field by designating two end zones about 70 yards apart, and sidelines about 40 yards apart. You also need a "ball"—either a glow stick or a tennis ball works well since they can be seen in the dark.

This game is played just like *Frisbee® Football* (see game rules in this book). Team A "kicks off" by throwing the *ball* (glow stick or tennis ball) to the opposing team. Team B throws the *ball* from player to player, with the goal of advancing down the field to score a touchdown. In this night version, players must catch the *ball* in their pillowcase. The catching player stops as soon as she has the ball and becomes the thrower (like in *Frisbee® Football,* players cannot run after making a catch). The catching player must take the ball out of her pillowcase and throw it to another teammate with her hand. The defending team must give the thrower a 3' space to throw from, but every other defender tries to intercept or knock down the *ball.* Turnovers occur when the *ball* is not caught, a defender intercepts or knocks the ball down with his pillowcase (only pillowcases are allowed, no arms or hands can be used), or someone catches out of bounds.

After a turnover, the other team starts at that point and goes in the opposite direction, trying to score a touchdown in their end zone. Each touchdown counts as one point. The scoring team then "kicks off" and play continues. The first team to score 10 points wins!

KICK THE CAN

 # OF PLAYERS: 4 or more
PLAYERS: Everyone!
OBJECTS NEEDED: Can or bucket

OR MORE

Divide players into teams of two. Begin by placing the can in the middle of the playing field or in the street. In this game, there are no boundaries. One team starts by being *it*—they count to 100 while all the other teams go to hide. Teammates can hide together or separate and hide individually. The goal is for both teammates from a team to run back and kick the can without being tagged by one of the players who is *it*.

After counting, *it* tries to find the hiding players. When players are found or spotted, they try to run back and *kick the can* before being tagged by *it*. Both teammates who are *it* can help tag a player, but they have to be careful because other players may make a run for the can while they are not looking. The hiding players do not necessarily need to be found—they just need to hide until they have a chance to go *kick the can* without being tagged. After a player does *kick the can,* they should place the can back in the original spot so that others coming to *kick the can* won't have to find it. If both players from a hiding team make it back to the can without being tagged, they receive four points (two points per player). If only one teammate *kicks the can*, that team only gets two points. If both players are tagged that team doesn't receive any points. The team that is *it* cannot closely guard the can—there is a 10' safe zone around the *can* that those that are *it* cannot enter. Once everyone has either been tagged, or *kicked the can,* then another round begins with a new team as *it.* The first team to score 15 points wins the game!

KICKBALL SQUARED

 # OF PLAYERS: 8 or more
PLAYERS: Everyone!
OBJECTS NEEDED: 2 Balls (large bouncy balls)

OR MORE

This new version of the classic game ramps up the fun with two people kicking at once! The game is played much like the way normal kickball is played (which is simply playing baseball, but the pitcher rolls a soft bouncy ball and the *batter* kicks the ball). Since two players are kicking, the pitcher rolls two balls at once for the pitch. The two players up to *bat* each kick a ball and simultaneously run the bases. However, the two teammates run the bases in *opposite* directions! One player runs the traditional route from 1st base to home base, while the other player runs to 3rd base first, then 2nd, to 1st, and then back home in order to score a point for the team.

Like baseball, and normal kickball, outs occur when a pop fly is caught, a runner is tagged by the ball, or the fielding team touches a base on a forced out. In this game, the fielding team can also throw the ball at the players running from base to base—if a ball hits a runner, it is an out. Two players can be at the same base at the same time. If a player gets three strikes or five foul balls, it is an out; and if one player kicks it and the other player strikes or kicks foul, the player who kicked still runs the bases. The team with the most points after five innings, or whichever team scores 30 runs first wins!

VARIATION: Rather than playing with two people kicking at once, play the traditional way with just one kicker at a time.

LIGHTNING BALL

OR MORE

 # OF PLAYERS: 2 or more
PLAYERS: Anna, Steven, Rachel, John
OBJECTS NEEDED: 2 Basketballs, Basketball Court

This basketball game is often referred to as *Speed*. Players stand at the free throw line in a single file line going away from the basket. The first two players in line each have a basketball. The first player starts by shooting to make a basket. Immediately following the first player's shot, the 2nd player in line shoots. The goal of the 2nd player is to sink his shot before the first person makes hers; and if this happens, the first person gets an out. Once a player receives two *outs,* that player is eliminated for that round and sits on the sidelines.

A player's first shot must be attempted from the free throw line. If she makes her shot, she gives her ball to the next person in line and then goes to the end of the line to wait for her next turn. If she misses her first shot, she shoots from anywhere (as close as she wants). For example, Anna shoots from the free throw line—if she makes the shot, she gets the rebound and quickly gives the ball to Rachel (the 3rd player in line). If she misses, she shoots from anywhere, but tries to make it before the next player makes his shot. Once Rachel gets a ball, she tries to make her shot before the next player makes his, and this continues down the line. If a player does not make a shot before the person behind her does, she gets an out. When a player receives two *outs* they leave for the rest of the round. The last person shooting wins that round, receives a point, and a new round begins. The first person to score three points wins. The winner chooses where everyone shoots from during the next round.

VARIATION: Play the game 'resurrection style.' In this version, players get only one out, but they get to come back into the game when the player who got them out gets out. If Anna gets Steven out—when someone else gets Steven out, then Anna comes back into the game. Thus, the game can only be won if one person gets everyone out.

VARIATION: To make this game even more fun, add two twists: W*agon Wheels* and *Bumps*. *Wagon Wheels* are when someone's ball is going through the hoop that could cause you to get an out, you throw your ball *up* through the net (in opposite direction—from the bottom up) to knock the other ball back out. *Bumps* allow you to bump another person's ball. You can only do a bump with your ball—no throwing or kicking, just use the ball to knock another player's ball away from the basket.

MIDNIGHT COMBAT

 # OF PLAYERS: 4 or more
PLAYERS: Rachel, Megan, Adam, John, Steven
OBJECTS NEEDED: Tennis Balls, Small Plastic Cups (have extra cups on hand in case any are ruined)

OR MORE

To begin, establish a 10' x 10' *home base* in the middle of the playing field. Each player needs a tennis ball and a small plastic cup. One player starts by being *it*. This player takes all the tennis balls and goes to hide. The others playing remain at *home base*. Without looking where *it* is going they count to 100 while *it* hides. After counting, the players each take a cup, separate and try to find *it*. Players do not want to search together in this game.

As players look for *it*, the player who is *it* can move around. *It* does not have to stay in the same place—she can move quietly whenever she likes and she *should* move after each player finds her. When someone finds *it*, then *it* gives that player a tennis ball. The player places the tennis ball on his cup like a torch, and then tries to return safely to *home base* without being caught.

Every player's goal is to be the first one to return to *home base* safely with a tennis ball—so everyone else is trying to prevent players from returning to *home base*. Once a player gets a tennis ball, he can either make a mad dash back to *home base* or try to sneak back without been seen. (Ideally, the cups are just the right size so the ball rests on top in plain sight, but is still securely held by the cup so it does not fall when players run).

When a player runs with a tennis ball, he cannot hold the ball or cover it in any way. The ball must always be visible, and like a torch, players must hold it at arms length (no hiding, holding or covering the ball is allowed). This is important since players are trying to find *it* while watching for players carrying balls. When a player sees a person with a ball, she tries to knock the ball off that player's cup before he safely returns to *home base*. The player with the ball can run and do whatever necessary to get to *home base*, but do so carefully so that his ball does not fall off his cup. If a ball does come off a player's cup—whether it falls off or is knocked off by another player—that person is out for that round and must sit near *home base* until a new round starts.

When players attempt to knock a ball off another player's cup, they can only knock the ball—no pushing, hitting, holding or tripping the player is allowed. The first player to make it to *home base* with the ball on the cup receives five points. Play continues as others keep trying to find *it*. The next player to successfully get *home* receives three points, and the 3rd player receives one point. If more are playing, then once three players make it to *home base* successfully, that round is over. Start another round and everyone takes a turn being *it*. The first player to score 15 points is the winner!

MULTIPLE LEGGED RACE

 # OF PLAYERS: 6 or more
PLAYERS: Everyone!
OBJECTS NEEDED: String or rope

OR MORE

The traditional 3-legged race pales in comparison to the excitement of this new version of the relay! Divide players into two equal teams and establish a starting line and middle line about 30' apart. Each team splits so that half of the team is at the starting line, and the other half are at the middle line. Each player needs a string that is roughly 12-18 inches long.

At "Go," one player from each team races from the starting line to the middle line. When a player arrives at the middle line, a teammate takes her string and ties one of her legs to the teammate that just arrived to form *three* legs. Tied together they run back to the starting line as quickly as possible. At the starting line, the next teammate takes his string and ties it to one of the legs of the two teammates already tied together—either player's leg will work. Then, all three teammates race back to the middle line. Players keep tying onto teammates until every player on the team is tied together and they all make it back to the starting line. Should a string come untied, the team must stop immediately and re-tie it before continuing. The first team to complete the relay is the winner!

VARIATION: Rather than the whole team being tied together, each player on a team pairs with another teammate. At "Go," one pair ties themselves together, runs to the middle line and back, and tags the next pair. That pair ties themselves together (not before), and goes down and back. This continues until one of the teams gets every pair down and back to win!

MURDERER IN THE DARK

 # OF PLAYERS: 6 or more
PLAYERS: Everyone!
OBJECTS NEEDED: Deck of Cards

OR MORE

Begin by removing all the Aces except for the Ace♥ from a deck of cards. Shuffle the remaining cards and deal them evenly to the players. Players look at their own cards and cannot reveal them to anyone else. The player with the Ace is the *Murderer*, and none of the other cards matter. The game can be played in the house with the lights off, or outside at night in a very dark place. Regardless of where the game is played, designate boundaries so that players can only enter certain rooms or limit the outside area to roughly 50 x 50 yards.

Players scatter and remain as quiet and unseen as possible. Players do not necessarily hide. In fact, they should not hide behind objects that would conceal them—they should simply scatter and move amongst each other in the dark. As everyone moves, the *Murderer's* objective is to kill everyone before being killed—everyone else wants to discover the *Murderer's* identity and kill him. Players cannot group together or hide with each other.

Players are killed when the *Murderer* comes nearby and quietly says, "You are dead," without anyone else hearing (the *Murderer* can only kill one player at a time). The player that just got killed must stop where she is—she must not move or speak. Everyone else quietly moves around trying to find dead people. If someone comes across another individual, he simply asks, "Are you dead?" That person must answer honestly by simply saying, "Yes" or "No." If the player says "No," she continues to move around looking for dead people. If, however, someone finds a dead player, the person who found the dead player yells, "Murderer in the dark!"

At this point, everyone comes back together—turn on the lights or have everyone gather at a predetermined location. Everyone the *Murderer* silently killed is out and cannot talk or participate for the rest of that round (thus not revealing who the *Murderer* is). The remaining players discuss and debate who they think the *Murderer* is. After a few minutes of conversation and accusations, a vote is held and the player with the most votes must "die." During the accusations, the *Murderer* pretends he is not the *Murderer*. If an innocent player receives the most votes, she is out for that round. If, however, they correctly kill the *Murderer*, that round is over. Thus, those that are not the *Murderer* have an incentive to find those that are dead quickly to prevent the *Murderer* from killing many players.

If the *Murderer* was not revealed, the remaining players scatter again and the *Murderer* starts killing people silently. Play continues until everyone correctly votes and kills the *Murderer*, or everyone else is either killed by the *Murderer* or innocently through the votes of others. Start another round by dealing out the cards again to determine a new *Murderer*.

OVER-UNDER SHOWDOWN

 # OF PLAYERS: 8 or more
PLAYERS: Everyone!
OBJECTS NEEDED: Two Balls

OR MORE

Divide players into two equal teams. Each team starts by lining up in a single file line with about 2' between teammates. The first players in each line hold a ball. At "Go," each team passes its ball back to the last teammate in line in this pattern:

- The first player faces forward and hands the ball to the player behind. him by bringing the ball up over his head and reaching back to hand it to the next player in line.
- The second player grabs the ball and passes the ball between her legs to the next teammate.
- The third player passes the ball over his head.
- The fourth player passes under her legs, etc.

Once the last person in line gets the ball, he races to the front of the line, and the passing pattern is repeated until the player that started the relay gets back to the front of the line again. The team that finishes fastest receives one point. Start another round and think of new ways to pass the ball. The first team to score three points wins!

PING PONG KILL

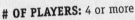

 # OF PLAYERS: 4 or more

PLAYERS: Adam, John, Rachel, Anna

OBJECTS NEEDED: Two Ping-Pong Tables, 4 Paddles, Ping-Pong Balls

Unlike most games in this book, this extremely fun version of ping-pong requires two very specific things—2 ping-pong tables! Set up the two tables side by side, leaving about one foot of space between the tables. One player stands at the end of each table (four players will play at once—one at each end of the tables). Each of these four players has a ping-pong paddle, and one ball is hit back and forth. Designate one place as the *King* spot—it is the spot everyone wants to move up to since it is the best!

The player at the *King* spot starts the game by serving the ball diagonally to the player on the other table (the ball bounces on her side, crosses over to the other table and bounces on the player's side diagonal from the server). After the serve, however, players can hit the ball in any direction and onto any side of any table. If the ball lands off the table, or hits the net before bouncing on another side, the player who made the bad shot is out. (At this point, if there are only four playing, the person who made a mistake goes to the last spot and everyone else moves up a spot. If more than four are playing, a new person rotates in and the person who made the mistake goes to the end of the line).

The four players compete against each other, trying to move to the *King* spot. If a player remains *King* for three consecutive plays, he receives one point (A "play" ends when someone makes a mistake. If the *King* did not make the mistake, he remained *King* for one play). The first player to score 10 points is the winner!

QUICKSAND MATCH

OR MORE

 # OF PLAYERS: 8 or more

PLAYERS: Everyone!

OBJECTS NEEDED: Random Objects: shirt, bag, pillow, short 2 x 4, etc.

Divide players into two teams (or teams of 6 - 8 players). Each team needs its own set of random objects. Examples of objects include books, sweaters, pillows, doormats, short 2 x 4s, bags, etc. Objects need to be small enough that at least two people could comfortably fit on one, but no more than three. Each team needs half as many objects as there are players on the team—if there are 10 on a team, the team needs five objects. If there are six on a team, they need three, etc. To begin, establish a starting line and a finish line about 50' apart. The goal is to be the first team across the finish line—without touching the ground!

At "Go," each team throws an object onto the ground about 3' to 4' from the starting line. Each team's first player stands on the object without touching the ground to get to it. A teammate hands the first player another object, whereupon the player throws it a little farther from where she is. She steps to the new object and her teammates begin standing on their team's objects. One or more teammates can stand on an object as long as no one touches the ground getting to it, or falls off the object(s) and touches the ground. Once any player crosses the starting line, he must always be standing on an object.

If any team member touches the ground for any reason, the entire team must start over. If a team has to start over, everyone must go back to the starting line, taking the objects with them. Slowly, teams start to advance down the playing field. Once every teammate is on the field, because objects are limited, the player(s) at the end have to pass objects to the front so the team can keep advancing. The first team to get every teammate across the finish line receives one point. Start another round, but add a twist. Be creative! The first team to win three rounds is the winner!

Twists include:

- All players on any object must be standing on one foot at all times—

- if another team sees two feet down, the entire team starts over.
- Only girls can stand on an object together.
- Only boys can stand on an object together.
- Every other object can only have one person on it at a time.

RANDOM RELAY

 # OF PLAYERS: 8 or more
PLAYERS: Everyone!
OBJECTS NEEDED: Nothing

OR MORE

This relay race may be random, but it is extremely fun! Divide players into two equal teams. Establish a *starting line* and a *middle line* about 30' away. Teams line up along the *starting line*. Players collaborate to decide what players must do for each leg of the relay. Players may decide to walk to the *middle line* and back on their knees, crab walk, run backward, do summersaults, do cartwheels, hop on one foot, bite into an apple and not let it fall, run down and back eating a banana (the banana must be eaten before next player can go), run down and place head on a bat and spin seven times and come back, blow up balloon and hit it down and back, etc. It can be absolutely anything...the more creative the better!

Each teammate in the relay must do a different, random action down to the *middle line* and back. Once back, he tags the next teammate, who does her random act down and back. The first team to get every player down and back receives one point. Rounds continue with more random acts, but have teammates go in pairs doing the random act down and back together (the next pair can't go until both are back). The first team to win three rounds wins!

VARIATION: Do this same relay, but with a sports twist! Examples of some random sports activities to do for each leg of the race include making a shot on the basketball court from a certain place, throwing a football and hitting a target, kicking a ball into a designated goal, bumping a volleyball into the hoop (or a bucket), running through an obstacle course, etc.

SHOE FRENZY

OR MORE

 # OF PLAYERS: 6 or more
PLAYERS: Everyone!
OBJECTS NEEDED: A pair of shoes for each player

Divide players into two teams. Players remove their shoes and place them in a large pile about 30' from the *starting line*. Mix up the pile of shoes to separate pairs. Have the teams line up at the starting line. At "Go," one player from each team races to the pile and searches for her matching pair of shoes. Once she has found both shoes, she must put them on (a player must tie or strap on the shoe properly before leaving), and then run back to tag the next teammate. The next player on the team runs to find his shoes, puts them on, and runs back to tag the next teammate. The first team to have all its players back with their shoes on and tied properly wins!

VARIATION: Shoe Shot Put: Designate a box that is roughly 10 x 10 yards. Form a throwing line about 15 yards from the box—teams will kick off their shoes from this line toward the box. Players should loosely place on their shoes so that they can easily kick them off. One player from each team goes first by kicking her shoes (one at a time) toward the middle box. Players receive a point for each shoe that lands inside the box. Players from each team take turns and get three attempts each. The team with the most points once everyone has gone wins!

SQUARE OF CHAOS

 # OF PLAYERS: 12 or more
PLAYERS: Everyone!
OBJECTS NEEDED: Chairs

Divide players into teams of six (adapt accordingly for more or less players). Place 12 chairs in a 20' square facing each other—there should be four 20' sides with three chairs on each side. Each team will start by having three teammates sit on three chairs side by side—sitting directly across from them are their three teammates.

At "Go," one player from each team races across the middle of the square to tag a teammate on the other side. Once this player is tagged, he runs across and tags his next teammate. This continues back and forth until it gets back to the first player, who then crosses in a different way (it could be crab walking, walking backward, crawling on hands and knees, etc). This goes back and forth for four different variations/crossings. For instance, in our game the players crossed like this:

- First crossing—players ran across normally.
- Second crossing—players walked across backward.
- Third crossing—players crawled on their hands and knees.
- Fourth crossing—players crab walked.
- Final crossing—all the players on one side simultaneously crossed to the other side.

The crossing teammate takes the seat of the tagged player that is racing to tag another teammate on the other side. This relay continues back and forth until everyone has had a turn going across the middle in the specified ways. The first team to complete all the crossings wins that round and receives a point. (There are often collisions in the middle—players cannot push or shove—so be careful!) Start another round, and make up different ways that people have to cross the middle section (i.e. hopping, running backwards, on their knees, spinning, etc.—it can be anything). The first team to win three rounds of relays is the winner!

VARIATION: Rather than using chairs, set up the playing field by establishing a large square about 15 x 15 yards long on all sides. Divide players into four teams—each team starts in a corner. Instead of players going back and forth tagging each other in the relay, one player at a time runs to the diagonal corner opposite of them and back. The next player does the same, but in a different way (crab walk, hop, walk on knees, run backward, etc.). You can even have 2 - 3 teammates crossing at the same time!

SUMMER'S BATTLE

 # OF PLAYERS: 6 or more
PLAYERS: Anna, Sarah, John, Steven, Megan, Kyle
OBJECTS NEEDED: 10 Chairs, 10 Large Plastic Cups, Water Balloons

OR MORE

Divide players into two equal teams. Designate a large area roughly 20 x 20 yards square that is split in half by establishing a clear *middle line* to separate the teams. Each team needs five chairs and five large plastic cups. Place five chairs along the far (back) baseline on each team's side—chairs should be roughly 7' apart. Put a large plastic cup on each chair. The goal is to be the first team to knock over the opposing team's five cups. How? By throwing water balloons!

Fill roughly 50-100 water balloons and divide them evenly between the teams. At "Go," teams throw water balloons to attempt to knock over the other team's cups. While doing so, they also try to protect their own cups from being knocked over. Players can do anything necessary to stop a water balloon from hitting a cup—it does not matter if players get hit with water balloons on their own side. The one rule however, is that players cannot closely guard the cups. To prevent this, there is a 5' section in front of the chairs, on both sides, that no player can enter.

Players can venture onto the opponent's side to get a closer aim and range at the cups, but if a player is hit with a water balloon while on the opponent's side, that person is *out*. When a player is *out*, he must sit on the sidelines until the next round. Players can also sneak over and steal the other team's water balloons, but again, if they get hit doing so, they are *out*. The first team to get everyone on the opposing team *out* or to knock over all five of the opponent's cups wins the round and receives one point. Start another round—the first team to win three rounds is the winner!

SWEDISH BOWLING

OR MORE

 # OF PLAYERS: 2 or more

PLAYERS: Anna, Adam, Rachel, Kyle

OBJECTS NEEDED: 9 Large Plastic Cups, 5 Tennis Balls, Frisbee®

This challenging, fun game is improvised from a popular Swedish game. It can be played in a gym or outdoors. Set up the playing field as follows:

- Place 4 plastic cups in a horizontal line about 7' apart.
- About 25'-30' away, place the opponent's 4 plastic cups in a horizontal line about 7' apart (parallel to the other team's 4 cups).
- Place the last cup directly in the middle between each team's 4 cups (this is the *middle cup*).
- Each team's 4 cups should be roughly 30' apart, and the *middle cup* should be 15' away in the middle of the team cups.

Divide players into two teams. Team A starts by taking the Frisbee® and tossing it into the playing field between both team's cups. When tossing, players stand behind their row of 4 cups and the Frisbee® must go beyond the *middle cup*. For each round, a team tosses five tennis balls from behind the team's row of 4 cups. To begin, one player on Team A takes a turn tossing a ball—she must first hit the Frisbee® her team just tossed out. Once the Frisbee® has been hit, then Team A tries to hit the other team's 4 cups. It may take Team A all five throws to hit the Frisbee®, but the Frisbee® must be hit before a team can attempt to hit their opponent's four cups. (Players can toss, roll, bounce or throw the ball—they are simply trying to hit the cup any way they can. Also, when a ball hits the Frisbee® or a cup, it just needs to clearly hit the cup, not necessarily knock it over.)

Once Team A has thrown five tennis balls, it is Team B's turn—they repeat what Team A did. It is important to note that if a team doesn't hit the Frisbee® in five throws, that team is finished for that round and it is the next team's turn. Each player should have a chance to make the tosses/throws. As the rounds progress, team's cups will be hit—once a cup is hit, remove it from play. After a team has hit all four of their opponent's cups, they need to hit the last cup—the *middle cup*—in order to win the game. When a team reaches this point, rather than having five attempts to hit the *middle cup* per turn, teams only have two attempts per turn. The team that hits the *middle cup* first wins that round. Set up play again and the first team to win three rounds is the winner!

TAPE BATTLE

 # OF PLAYERS: 6 or more
PLAYERS: Megan, Sarah, Anna, Adam, Rachel, Kyle
OBJECTS NEEDED: 2 Rolls of Tape, 2 Chairs

OR MORE

Establish a playing field in a gym or outdoors that is roughly 20 x 20 yards square. Set up a *safety zone* in two of the four corners—these zones should be in opposite corners. The *safety zones* are simply a 5' radius circle. Place two chairs inside each *safety zone*. In preparation, rip off about 30 small pieces of tape and stick them onto the two chairs in each *safety zone*.

Players compete against each other. Each player starts with one piece of tape in hand, and players spread throughout the playing field. At "Go," the goal is to place a piece of tape on the back of another player, while avoiding having someone put a piece of tape on you. For a piece of tape to count, it has to be placed on a player's back (arms, legs, stomach, etc. do not count). Once a player has placed a piece of tape on someone else, he runs to the *safety zone* (while still trying to avoid being taped by others) and grabs another piece of tape. Players can only have two pieces of tape in hand at all times.

When a player is in the *safety zone,* he cannot be taped by another player, and there should be a 10' barrier around each *safety zone* so that others do not closely guard the *zones.* Players can only be in a *safety zone* and the surrounding barrier for 10 seconds. Players cannot deflect others trying to tape them, nor can they push or shove—they can only run away or maneuver to avoid being taped. At the end of a designated time, whoever has the least amount of pieces of tape on his or her back wins that round and receives a point. Remove the pieces of tape and start another round. The first player to win three rounds is the winner!

TEAM MARCO POLO

OR MORE

 # OF PLAYERS: 6 or more
PLAYERS: Adam, Rachel, Kyle, Megan, Steven, John
OBJECTS NEEDED: Swimming Pool

The classic game of *Marco Polo* is now more competitive—and much more fun! Divide players into pairs. One pair starts by being *it.* Both players who are *it* must close their eyes while the other pairs quietly swim away. After a few seconds, the pair that is *it* yells, "Marco," and every other person playing must answer by yelling, "Polo." The *it* pair keeps their eyes closed and swims around trying to tag other players. When players are tagged by *it,* they are out and must sit on the sideline.

As the game progresses, *it* continues to call out "Marco," and everyone responds with "Polo" each time. Players cannot get out of the swimming pool to get away from *it,* and *it* cannot open their eyes at all. The last player tagged receives three points, and the next to last player tagged receives one point. Each pair should try to be the last two people in the game so they can score the most points. Start another round so each pair has a turn being *it.* The first team to score 15 points wins!

THE PURSUIT

 # OF PLAYERS: 6 or more
PLAYERS: Everyone
OBJECTS NEEDED: 2 Flashlights

Play this night game in a field or a park, or even in a neighborhood between homes and in the street. In the middle of the playing area, designate a 10' x 10' section as *home base*. Divide players into teams of two. One team starts by being *it*. To begin each round, a category is chosen. Categories can be anything: U.S. cities, presidents, sports, fruits, countries, cars, etc. The two players who are *it* both need a flashlight. They start by counting to 100 while the remaining players go and hide. The other teams can either hide together or separate and hide individually.

After counting, the *it* players search for the hiding players using their flashlights (they can search together or separate). The hiding players can either stay hidden in one place or move around quietly to avoid being found. Eventually, *it* will spot people hiding or moving around. When the *it* players see someone, they will shine their flashlights on that person. The goal for *it* is to quickly shine their lights in the player's face, and then tag that player before he can return to *home base* safely. When *it* shines their lights in a player's face, players cannot block their faces or hide in any way once the light touches them. In fact, once the light touches any part of a player's body, he must stop where he is. The goal for the person who has been illuminated by the flashlight is to name something from the previously chosen category before *it's* light reaches his face.

For example, if the category chosen was *U.S. Cities*—when *it* finds Kyle and shines a light on him, Kyle must stop and before the light hits his face, he must quickly yell the name of any U.S. city. If Kyle yells a city before the light reveals his face, he is safe and gets to continue running around and hiding from *it*. If this does happen, *it* must pursue someone else—neither of the *it* pair can shine the light on Kyle until they have spotted someone else first. However, if the light does hit and reveal Kyle's face before he says something from the category—then the race is on! Kyle has no choice—he must try to run back to *home base* before being tagged by *it* (both players who are *it* can work together to try to tag Kyle).

It is possible for two people (at the most) to be running back to *home base* at the same time if the two who are *it* separated and are individually finding and tagging players.

If a player is found, his face revealed and he is tagged by *it* before reaching *home base* safely, he is out for that round and must sit near *home base* until the round is over. Players cannot run to *home base* unless they are spotted with the flashlight and fail to say a category fast enough. If a player notices that her teammate is caught and being chased, she cannot help in any way or purposely reveal herself to distract *it* from tagging her teammate. Any player that reaches *home base* without being tagged receives a point. The goal is for both players from a team to score two points per round. Once everyone has either been tagged or made it to *home base* safely, start another round with a new team being *it*. A team that is *it* does not score points, but tries to prevent other teams from obtaining points. The team with the most points after every team has taken a turn being *it* wins. Other alternatives are to declare the winner after a designated time or decide that the first team to reach a set number of points is the winner.

VARIATION: Rather than naming a category, when players are spotted they try to make it to *home base*. The light does not have to hit their faces and there are no categories—the goal is just to get to *home base* before being tagged by *it*.

TRIANGULAR TEAM PICKLE

 # OF PLAYERS: 6 or more
PLAYERS: Everyone!
OBJECTS NEEDED: Frisbee®, 3 Shoes

OR MORE

The common game of baseball *Hot Box* or *Rundown* just got a little bit more challenging! Place three old shoes about 25' to 30' apart to form a triangle. The shoes are the bases. Players are on teams of two. One team begins as the *throwers* while the remaining players are the *runners*. All the *runners* start at the same base. The *runners* goal is to run from base to base without being tagged or hit by the Frisbee®. The *throwers* goal is to throw the Frisbee® back and forth between each other trying to tag or hit the *runners*.

The *runners* cannot run outside of certain boundaries. The *runners* and *throwers* can run around anywhere inside the three bases, but there is an imaginary line 10' past each base (surrounding the three bases) that a *runner* cannot run past (*throwers* can go outside the boundary to retrieve the Frisbee®). The two *throwers* work together to try and tag or hit the *runners* as they run from base to base. A *thrower* can tag a *runner* with the Frisbee® or throw the Frisbee® and hit a *runner*—but when a *runner* is on a base, she is safe and cannot be tagged or hit with the Frisbee®. A *runner* can only remain on a base for 10 seconds, and unlike baseball, there are no forced outs (a *thrower* can't just touch a base when a *runner* is coming—he must either tag the player with the Frisbee® or throw the Frisbee® at the *runner* and hit them). When a *runner* makes it all the way around the three bases, she receives a point.

When a *runner* is either tagged or hit with the Frisbee®, that *runner* receives one strike. After a *runner* receives two strikes, he is out for that round and must sit on the side until a new round starts. When the *throwers* get everyone out, the round is over and a new team (set of two) takes their turn being the *throwers*. At this point, each team adds up however many points were scored between the two teammates. For example, if one teammate made it around the bases three times, and the other teammate made it around five times, that team has eight points. Each team takes a turn being the *throwers*. The first team to score 50 points wins!

WATER BALLOON TOSS

 # OF PLAYERS: 8 or more
PLAYERS: Everyone!
OBJECTS NEEDED: Towels, Water Balloons

OR MORE

To prepare for this extremely fun—and wet—summer game, fill 30 to 40 balloons with water. Divide players into two teams. Each team needs two towels and a water balloon. Four players from each team start this fun tossing game. The object is to toss a water balloon back and forth between teammates using the towels to throw and catch the balloon. The four players on each team pair up and each player grabs the end of a towel (each player holds one of the short ends). The two pairs from each team with outstretched towels stand about 10' apart (with about 5' separating the two teams).

One pair from each team places a water balloon on one of the towels. Those two teammates must fling the balloon to their other two teammates, who try to catch the water balloon with their towel. After each successful throw and catch, each pair must take a step back—making the next throw more difficult. If the water balloon is not caught or it breaks, the team earns a strike and the pairs from that team take a step closer to each other. If the balloon breaks, simply get another balloon and start throwing again after moving a step closer.

For each round, teams are only allowed three strikes. Once a team gets its third strike, they stop where they are. If the other team is already farther apart—meaning the two pairs have moved farther than the team that just got three strikes—than the farthest team gets one point and wins the round. If the team still throwing is not farther, they keep throwing until they get their third strike. The team that advances the farthest before receiving three strikes is the winner for that round. Between rounds, the four players who beat their opponents get to have a little extra fun! The four players that lost must line up side by side with about 3' to 4' between the players. The four winners stand roughly 30' away, and each winning player gets to throw one water balloon at the four losing teammates. Those on the losing team must stand in one place and cannot dodge the water balloons. If a player successfully throws and hits a player on the losing team, she earns one point (which is added to the team's total points).

If there are more than four on each team, the other teammates rotate in and start another round (otherwise the same people continue playing). The team that scores 20 points first wins!

WATER BALLOON VOLLEYBALL

 # OF PLAYERS: 8 or more
PLAYERS: Everyone!
OBJECTS NEEDED: Water Balloons, Towels, Volleyball Net

OR MORE

Play this game at an outdoor volleyball court, in a gym, or simply set up a net by tying string between two trees. In preparation, fill up quite a few water balloons. Split players into two teams and then divide each team's players into pairs. Each pair holds a towel so that it is stretched between the two players. The four players on each team pair up and each player grabs the end of a towel (each player holds one of the short ends). Teams stand on their respective sides of the volleyball court and then spread their players (with their towels) on the court.

Using a water balloon as the ball, players (each pair) use their towels to fling it back and forth over the net. Once a pair catches it in their towel, they fling it back to the opponent's side. Like normal volleyball, a point is scored when the ball (balloon) touches the ground or goes out of bounds. Unlike volleyball rules, rather than getting three hits per side, teams only have one hit (throw). If a balloon breaks as a pair is catching it or throwing it, that also counts as a point for the opponent. Simply replace broken water balloons with new ones as needed. Players cannot touch the balloon with any part of their bodies—just the towel. Play continues until one team scores 25 points to win!

WATER LAUNCH

 # OF PLAYERS: 4 or more
PLAYERS: Adam, Kyle, Anna, Rachel
OBJECTS NEEDED: Water Balloons, Buckets

OR MORE

Fill roughly 100 balloons with water. Divide players into pairs—one person from each pair is the *thrower* and the other is the *catcher*. Establish a throwing line for where the *throwers* stand. Then establish a 10' x 10' box for each pair that are side by side. The 10' x 10' boxes are in a horizontal row parallel to the throwing line, with about 5' to 10' between each box. The *catchers* stand in their respective boxes with a bucket and each *thrower* stands on the line directly across from his partner's box. Each *thrower* starts with five water balloons.

Each *thrower* gets five throws, and will toss the water balloons to the *catcher* in the box. The *catcher* tries to catch the water balloon(s) in the bucket and keep as much water in the bucket as possible. *Catchers* cannot leave the box when attempting to catch a balloon—if the *catcher* leaves the box to catch a balloon it doesn't count. After the five throws, each pair switches places, and the new *thrower* tosses five water balloons to her partner. After those five throws, each pair empties their buckets of water into a different team bucket (to hold water between throws). Players switch roles again and start another round doing the same thing. The pair that has the most water in their team bucket after each player has thrown three times is the winner. Use a ruler or yardstick to measure the water.

WET RELAY

 # OF PLAYERS: 6 or more
PLAYERS: Everyone!

OR MORE

OBJECTS NEEDED: 2 Chairs, 2 Measuring Cups, 2 Bowls, 2 Cups, 2 Spoons, 2 Plates, 2 Cookie Sheets, Bucket of Water, Water Balloons

Establish a start line and a finish line about 30' apart. Place a chair for each team at the finish line, and on each chair place a large glass measuring cup. Put a bucket of water at the start line for each team, along with the other random objects to be used to transport the water from one end to the other (see above). Divide players into two equal teams and line up each team at the starting line.

At "Go," a player from each team grabs the team cup and starts filling the team cookie sheet with water. Once it is full, the first two players rush to the finish line and dump the water (or whatever remains) from the cookie sheet into the team measuring cup. Since this is a relay race, players are trying to do this as fast as possible. Once the first player dumps his water, he rushes back to the start line to tag the next player in line. The next player must fill up a plate with water, run it to the finish line, dump it and return to tag a teammate. This continues with each player running a different leg of the relay. Examples of various ways to transport the water include:

- Drink from the cup, transport the water by mouth and spit it into the measuring cup.
- Cup both hands and fill them with water.
- Fill a small or large wooden spoon with water.
- Fill a bowl with water and run down.

There can be as many legs of the relay as everyone decides, even if that means players go more than once.

The team that finishes first receives three points, but the team that has the most water in their measuring cup receives five points. Start another round and add a little twist each round. Still using the same objects to transport the water, make an obstacle course by putting random tables, chairs, garbage cans, etc. in the way. For round three, each player can do three random actions on the way to the measuring cup (with or without the obstacles in the way). Examples include bending down to pick up a ball and throwing it with your opposite hand, crawling under a chair, lying down on the ground, doing a sit-up, etc. The next round, players from each team can line up from one end to the other and pass as much water from the bucket down the line in a human chain. The first team to overflow their measuring cup wins three points for that round. After all the rounds are over, the team with the most points wins!

VARIATION: Between each round, the winning team gets to throw water balloons at the losers. Each person on the losing team lines up side by side with about 3' between players. Those on the losing team cannot dodge the balloons or duck. Each player on the winning team gets one throw. For every player hit, the winning team gets one more point added to its total score.

WINTER WARFARE

 # OF PLAYERS: 6 or more

PLAYERS: Adam, Rachel, Kyle, Anna, John, Megan

OBJECTS NEEDED: Snow, 6 Chairs, 6 Large Plastic Cups

OR MORE

Divide players into two equal teams. There are no boundaries for this warfare, but a *middle line* separates the team's sides. Each team takes three chairs and places them in a row side by side about 10' apart. The chairs for both teams should be about 30' from the *middle line* (parallel to the *middle line)*. On each chair, teams place a large plastic cup. Both teams need a *jail*, which can simply be a 10' x 10' area about 20' from the *middle line*. Lastly, teams should prepare many snowballs and go to their respective sides. Let the battle begin!

The goal for each team is to be the first to knock over the other team's three cups, while protecting their own cups from being knocked over. To prevent the cups from being closely guarded, an invisible 5' barrier surrounds the chairs and no player can enter that area (when protecting or throwing). Players throw snowballs back and forth trying to knock over their opponent's cups. If a player is hit with a snowball on his own side, it does not matter. However, players can venture onto their opponent's side to get a closer aim at the cups. This is completely legal, but if a player is hit with a snowball while on the opponent's side, that player must go to jail.

A player can be released from *jail* by another teammate by simply having that teammate tag him while he is in *jail*. Only one person can be released from *jail* at a time, and both players must return to their side before throwing snowballs at the opponent's cups. Play continues, and the team that knocks over their opponent's cups first receives one point. Another round begins and the first team to score three points wins!

7 ON THE LINE

 # OF PLAYERS: 2 or more
PLAYERS: Adam, Rachel, Anna, John
OBJECTS NEEDED: Basketball, Basketball Hoop

OR MORE

In a gym, backyard basketball hoop, or at a nearby park, this basketball game reveals the best free throw shooter! One player starts by shooting the ball from the free throw line to make a goal. There is always at least "one on the line" in this game. When a player misses a shot, he gets one point. In this game, points are not good! For example, if Adam shoots and misses, he receives one point. The next person shoots. If she makes it, then there is now "two on the line." If three people make their shots, there's "four on the line." If the next person misses her shot, she receives four points and the count goes back to "one on the line." A player always receives at least one point for every shot missed.

Play continues with each person taking a turn shooting—if only two people are playing, they simply alternate shots. Once a player reaches seven points, he is out for that round. The last person shooting wins that round and receives one point (this is a good point). Start another round and the first person to win three rounds is the winner!

CHILDREN'S GAMES
·········· INDOORS ··········

BEST ENDING

 # OF PLAYERS: 3 or more
PLAYERS: Alyssa, Justin, Hannah
OBJECTS NEEDED: Nothing

OR MORE

Creativity and imagination make this storytelling game fun and fascinating! One player begins by telling a relatively short story (30 seconds to a minute) about absolutely anything. This player tells the story aloud to all the players— but leaves off the end of the story. The goal is to tell the best ending so other players vote for your story's ending.

At this point, every other player takes about 30 seconds to think of his own ending to the story. Going in a circle to the left, each player tells the group her version of the story's ending. Everyone's version should only be 20 - 30 seconds long. Once each person takes a turn, everyone votes on whose ending was the best (most creative or funny). Players cannot vote for their own endings. The player receiving the most votes earns a point. The winning player begins another round by telling a new story. Play continues round after round. The first player to score three points is the winner!

CHAIN OF NUMBERS

 # OF PLAYERS: 2 or more
PLAYERS: Ashley, Ryan, Eric
OBJECTS NEEDED: Deck of Cards

OR MORE

Deal all the cards evenly to the players. Players look at their cards and arrange them by suit and in numerical order. Players can only play a card that is one higher/lower in the same suit as a card previously played or one that is the same numerical value in another suit. Players take turns and whoever has the 7♥ begins by playing it in the center. In our game, Ashley played the 7♥, so the next player can play a 6♥ or an 8♥, or a 7 of another suit.

If Ryan plays 6♥, he would place it under the 7♥ because it is a lower card. If Ryan plays the 8♥, he would place it above the 7♥ because it is higher in value and of the same suit. A 7 of another suit would be placed on the side of the 7♥. After the player places a card, the next player gets a turn. Eric can play by the 7♥, or by the new card just played. If the new card was a 6♥, Eric can play the 5♥ below the 6♥, or a 6 of any other suit to the side. If he does not have a card that will play on his turn, he must pass and lose that turn. Play continues around the circle. The first player to get rid of all of his cards receives three points, the next player to get rid of his cards receives two points, the third player receives one point and the round is over. Start another round, reshuffle and deal again. Play continues until one player reaches 20 points to win the game!

CONNECT THE DOTS CONTEST

OR MORE

 # OF PLAYERS: 2 or more
PLAYERS: Aubrey, Nicole
OBJECTS NEEDED: Paper, Pencils

Draw 64 small dots on a piece of paper in a specific pattern—8 rows by 8 columns with spaces between each dot. Each player needs a pencil. The goal is to connect the dots to form squares—and to have the most completed squares once all the dots have been connected!

Aubrey begins by drawing a line connecting any two dots. Drawn lines can go sideways, or up and down—but not diagonal. Nicole takes her turn and does the same. At first, players just alternate turns drawing lines. As the game progresses and more lines are drawn, players will notice places that drawing a line will either complete a square or potentially allow the other player to form a square. When a player draws a line that completes a square, she puts her initials in that box (signifying she won the box by completing the square). Whenever a player completes a box, she gets to go again. Players continue to alternate back and forth until each dot has been connected and every possible move has been made. The player with the most squares filled with her initials wins!

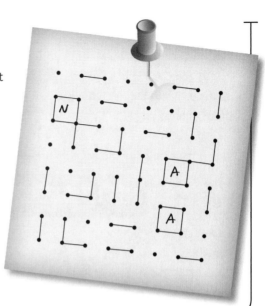

GO FISH

OR MORE

 # OF PLAYERS: 2 or more
PLAYERS: Jacob, Andrew
OBJECTS NEEDED: Deck of Cards

This classic children's game is best played with actual *Go Fish* cards—however, you can improvise with a normal deck if necessary. Begin by dealing six cards to each player, and placing the remaining cards in a pile face down in the center. Each player lays down any pairs he already has (a pair is two cards of the same numerical value: two 7s, two 3s, two Kings, etc.). Play begins with the person to the left of the dealer asking any other player for a certain card—the goal is to collect pairs. If the player asked does have the requested card, he must hand it over, then the player who asked for it takes the pair and places it to the side. When a player makes a pair, he gets to go again.

If the player asked does not have the requested card, he says, *"Go Fish!"* The player who asked draws a card from the center pile, and it is then the next player's turn. Play continues around the circle until one player matches every card in his hand and no longer has any cards to play—he receives three points.

Play continues, and the next player to get rid of all his cards receives two points, and the 3rd player receives one point. At this point, the round is over! Start another round, reshuffle and deal again. The first player to score 20 points is the winner!

GOLF BALL BILLIARDS

 # OF PLAYERS: 2 or more
PLAYERS: Andrew, Justin
OBJECTS NEEDED: 10 Golf Balls, Pencils

OR MORE

Mark a circle on a flat surface that is about 3' in diameter. The surface can be carpet, tile, or cement outside—simply mark the circle using yarn, string, or sidewalk chalk. Place 10 golf balls very close to each other in the center of the circle, like normal billiard balls. Mark one of the balls as the cue ball. Each player needs a pencil to use as a cue stick!

Players take turns hitting the cue ball with their pencils. The goal is to try and knock the other balls outside the circle. If a player's shot does knock another ball(s) outside the circle, he gets to go again. However, like normal billiards, on the next turn the cue ball must be hit from where it last stopped. Players cannot hit or touch another ball when hitting the cue ball except with the cue stick (pencil). Once a ball goes outside the circle, the player who hit it out places it by his side (it will equal one point at the end of the round). If a player's hit did not make a ball leave the circle, he loses his turn and it is the next player's turn. Also, if a player's shot makes the cue ball leave the circle, he loses his turn and any other ball that left does not count—it should be placed back in the center of the circle. Play continues until all nine balls have been knocked out of the circle (leaving only the cue ball inside it). Each player receives one point for every ball he knocked out for that round. Play continues with more rounds. The first player to score 25 points is the winner!

LUCKY GUESS

 # OF PLAYERS: 2 or more
PLAYERS: Ashley, Nicole, Alyssa, Aubrey
OBJECTS NEEDED: Deck of Cards

OR MORE

There is absolutely no skill involved in this fun game—just a lot of lucky guessing! Deal 6 - 8 cards to all players, and the players can look at their cards. Place the remaining cards face down in a pile in the center, and move one card face down next to the center pile. Play begins by having players choose any card they want from their hands. Players make a guess as to whether or not they think their chosen card is higher or lower than the card face down in the middle. Players that think their cards are higher place them in a designated "higher" pile above the face down card. Players that think their cards are lower place them in the designated "lower" pile beneath the face down card.

Once everyone has played her card, the middle card that is face down is revealed. The players who guessed correctly take back their cards and place them in their own "winning" piles next to them (players will not play these cards anymore). If a player guessed wrong, her card goes to the bottom of the middle pile. Play continues by taking the next card from the middle pile and again placing it face down, and everyone makes another guess. Once each person has played each of the cards in her hand, players receive one point for each card in their winning pile. Start another round—and the first person to 20 points wins!

LUCKY SPEED WRITER

 # OF PLAYERS: 2 or more
PLAYERS: Ryan, Hannah, Jacob, Aubrey
OBJECTS NEEDED: Papers, Pencils, Dice

OR MORE

Players need their own papers and pencils for this fast, fun game. The object of the game is to be the first player to write each number from 1-100, and then to be the first to score three points. Ryan starts by taking one dice and rolling until he gets a 6. It may take a few tries, but once he rolls a 6, the game is on!

After Ryan rolls a 6, he passes the dice to the player on his left—Hannah. It's now her turn to roll and she's trying to get a 6, too. When Ryan rolls his 6 and passes the dice, he uses his paper and pencil to start writing the numbers from 1 up to 100. He keeps writing until Hannah rolls a 6—once this happens, Ryan must immediately stop writing and wait for his next turn. Hannah starts writing while Jacob is trying to roll a 6, etc.

For example, if Ryan wrote the numbers 1 - 34, when it comes back to his turn he starts on 35 and keeps going up to 100. The first player to reach 100 receives a point. Then, start another round—but this time the person who started the last round goes last. Play continues round after round, and the first player to score five points, or win five rounds, is the winner!

MATCHING ANIMALS

 # OF PLAYERS: 3 or more
PLAYERS: Andrew, Nicole, Justin, Ashley
OBJECTS NEEDED: Deck of Cards

OR MORE

Each player chooses an animal to be identified by—it can be any animal, and animals change each round. Deal the entire deck of cards evenly between players—deal them face down and they should remain face down in a pile in front of each player. The player to the left of the dealer, Andrew, starts by turning over a card from his pile and placing it above (toward the center of) his pile of cards. The next player, Nicole, does the same, and this continues around the circle.

Everyone is looking for a match—a match is any card of the same numerical value (two 6s, two 8s, two Queens, etc). When a card is played that matches another card that is face up in any player's pile, the goal is to be the first person to yell the animal name of the other person whose card matches the one just played (not the person's animal who just played the card). If Andrew plays the match and has the animal name hippopotamus, and Justin is the player who has the other match and has the animal name kangaroo—then the first player to yell, "Kangaroo!" wins that match. The player who wins a match takes the two matching cards and places them in his winning pile.

As play continues around the circle, players keep flipping over cards and placing them side by side in front of them. Play gets harder because everyone has to keep track of many cards from many players. Once everyone has turned over every card, the round is over. Players receive a point for each match in their winning piles. Start another round by reshuffling and dealing again— but now every player must choose a new animal name. If a player calls the animal of a player from last round, he loses one of his matches. The first player to score 30 points is the winner!

MEMORY

 # OF PLAYERS: 2 or more
PLAYERS: Ashley, Jacob, Eric, Nicole
OBJECTS NEEDED: Deck of Cards

OR MORE

You need a sharp memory and some lucky guessing to win this competitive game! Begin by shuffling the cards well and dealing the entire deck face down in approximately seven rows and seven columns so each card has its own spot. Players take turns, and the player left of the dealer goes first. For each turn, a player turns over two random cards, hoping to find a match. A match is any two cards with the same numerical value (two 6s, two 3s, two Kings, etc).

When a player does find a match, she takes both cards and places them in a pile in front of her—and she gets to go again until she turns over two cards that do not match. If the two cards do not match, the player places them back in their spots, face down, and it is the next player's turn. Players try to remember where certain cards are that have been turned over so that when their turns come around again, they can choose a pair that matches. Play continues until there are no cards left—the player with the most matches once all the cards have been paired receives one point. Reshuffle, deal the cards face down again, and start another round. The player who wins three rounds first is the winner!

MUSICAL CHAIRS / SIMON SAYS TWIST

 # OF PLAYERS: 5 or more
PLAYERS: Everyone!
OBJECTS NEEDED: Chairs

OR MORE

Collect one chair less than the number of people playing—if there are seven people playing, gather six chairs. Place the chairs in a circle facing each other—but make the circle large enough so there is room to move around in the middle. One player starts by being *it*—she stands in the middle of the circle of chairs. The remaining players sit on a chair.

To begin, *it* says, "I like _____." *It* fills in the blank with whatever word she likes. However, players are specifically listening for words that start with one of these three letters—*I, J* or *K*. If *it* says a word that starts with one of those letters, then players must get out of their chairs, run across the circle and sit in a different chair. Players must choose a chair at least two chairs away from where they were sitting.

Why those three letters? Because they can easily be mistaken for other letters (like E, G or C). If *it* says a word that starts with an *E, G* or *C* and someone mistakenly stands—then the player who made the mistake becomes *it* in the middle. At times, more than one person may mistakenly stand—when that happens there's a race between the players who were mistaken to sit before everyone else. Keep in mind that *it* is also trying to sit down, so players need to be quick. Of course, *it* tries to throw people off! If any other word is said that does not start with the letters *I, J* or *K*—then players sit and wait for *it* to say a word starting with one of the right letters. When a player becomes *it*, he also receives a strike. Once a player receives three strikes, he is out. Every time a player gets out, remove a chair from the circle. The winner is the last person in the game!

NEW 20 QUESTIONS

 # OF PLAYERS: 3 or more
PLAYERS: Aubrey, Justin, Eric
OBJECTS NEEDED: Papers, Pencils

OR MORE

Much like the classic game of *20 Questions*, players take turns asking questions to discover what *it* is! One player begins by thinking of *it*—any noun (a person, place or thing) will work. The other players ask questions to narrow the possibilities. The questions asked cannot be open-ended—the answers must only be *yes* or *no*. Everyone collectively keeps track of how many questions have been asked and the rounds progress.

There's a great twist to this new way of playing! If Aubrey thinks she knows what *it* is, she writes what she thinks *it* is on her paper plus the number of questions the group had asked up until that point. For example, if the group had already asked 16 questions when Aubrey thinks she knows what *it* is, she'll write *DOG 16* on her paper. She also tells the group that she's writing her guess so that everyone else knows what question she was on when she guessed (this is done to prevent cheating).

Once a player writes her guess, she cannot participate or guess anymore during that round, nor can she change her guess. The remaining players keep asking questions until each player guesses what *it* is. Once everyone has discovered (or thinks they have discovered) what *it* is and written their answers, *it* is revealed. Players with correct guesses receive a point. Players with incorrect answers do not receive a point. Players also receive a point for every question asked after they correctly guessed. For example, if Eric was the last player to guess on the 35th question, then everyone who guessed correctly subtracts the number of his guess from 35 to find the number of extra points earned. Since Aubrey guessed on the 16th question, she receives an additional 19 points (35-16=19). Justin guessed on the 20th question so he gets 15 more points, etc. Thus, the sooner a player guesses, the more points she can earn. Start another round—everyone takes a turn being the one to choose a new *it*. After every player has taken a turn, the player with the most points is the winner!

NEW HIDE & GO SEEK

 # OF PLAYERS: 4 or more
PLAYERS: Alyssa, Eric, Jacob, Nicole
OBJECTS NEEDED: Nothing

A competitive twist updates this classic children's game! Divide players into teams of two. One team starts by being *it*—they count to 100 while the other teams go and hide. Teammates, however, do not want to hide together—they should separate and hide individually. After counting, *it* goes to try and find players who are hiding. The last player found receives three points and the next to last player found receives one point—the other players do not earn points. Teammates try to be the last two people found so their team can score the most points. Each team takes a turn being *it*, and the first team to score 10 points wins!

OLD MAID

 # OF PLAYERS: 3 or more
PLAYERS: Hannah, Eric, Jacob, Ashley
OBJECTS NEEDED: Deck of Cards

OR MORE

Old Maid is a classic children's game that has its own cards, but a normal deck will work! Remove one Queen from a deck of cards, and then deal the remaining cards evenly to the players. The player to the left of the dealer, Hannah, starts by choosing one card from any other player's hand. The player who Hannah grabs a card from won't let her see the face of the cards—Hannah has to pick one without knowing what card she is choosing. Hannah can either keep the card or match it with another one of her cards and place the matched pair to the side. Matches are two cards with the same numerical value—two 3s, two 6s, two Kings, etc.

Next Eric chooses a card from any other player's hand. Play continues around the circle as players try to find matches for each card and quickly play all their cards. There is one extra Queen that is passed around—this is the Old Maid. Players do not want the Old Maid at any time, but especially at the end of the round! At first, players don't know which Queen is the Old Maid—the player who has it will know when her identity is revealed when the other pair of Queens is played. Play continues around the circle and eventually players find matches for all their cards. The player who has the Old Maid at the end of the round receives one strike. Reshuffle, start a new round and once a player receives two strikes, he is out of the game. The last player remaining after everyone else receives two strikes is the winner!

PAIRS

 # OF PLAYERS: 2 or more
PLAYERS: Alyssa, Ryan
OBJECTS NEEDED: Deck of Cards

OR MORE

Deal four cards to each player. Place six cards in the center face up. The remaining cards form a face down draw pile in the center. The player to the left of the dealer, Alyssa, starts by trying to pair the cards in her hand with one of the six cards in the center. Pairs are two cards of the same numerical value—two 5s, two Kings, etc. If Alyssa can match a card from her hand with one in the middle, she takes the middle card and her matching card and places them to the side. She will then draw another card from the draw pile so that she always has four cards in her hand. If a player has two or three cards in her hand that make pairs, she can match them all (and then draw however many cards necessary to keep four in her hand).

Play continues around the circle in this manner. If Ryan cannot match any cards in his hand with a middle card, he has to place one of his cards in the center. (The number of cards in the center will increase and decrease as the game progresses.) While Ryan can still pair up the cards in his hand on his next turns, he only keeps three cards in his hand from then on, etc. When a player runs out of his four cards, he is out. Players eventually run out of cards one by one. In the end, each player counts his pairs and players receive one point for each pair they got for that round. Reshuffle, deal again and start a new round with everyone—the first person to score 30 points is the winner!

PAY UP

 # OF PLAYERS: 2 or more
PLAYERS: Nicole, Ryan, Jacob, Hannah
OBJECTS NEEDED: Deck of Cards

OR MORE

Deal the entire deck evenly to the players. Players should leave their cards face down. Nicole starts by turning over the top card in her pile and placing it in the middle to form a discard pile. Ryan, Jacob and Hannah all do the same. What card is played is irrelevant unless it is an Ace, King, Queen or Jack. When one of those cards is played, the next player must *pay!*

Payment is made as follows:

- Ace—*pay* by placing 4 cards face up onto the discard pile
- King—*pay* by placing 3 cards face up onto the discard pile
- Queen—*pay* by placing 2 cards face up onto the discard pile
- Jack—*pay* by placing 1 card face up onto the discard pile

The person who played the Ace or face card will get to take the entire discard pile. However, if one of the "payment" cards is also a face card or an Ace, once that card is played, the next player (whose turn is next) must pay the person who was making a payment. This continues until someone's payment does not include a face card or an Ace, and the last person being "paid" takes the whole pile! Play continues until someone obtains the entire pile (or whoever has the most cards when *time* is called).

PENNY SEARCH

 # OF PLAYERS: 4 or more
PLAYERS: Ryan, Aubrey, Eric, Alyssa
OBJECTS NEEDED: Penny, Paper and Pencil for each player

OR MORE

To begin, all except one player should leave the room. While they're gone, one player hides a penny in the room. The placement of the penny needs to be relatively difficult to find, but players should be able to see it without moving anything. Once the penny has been placed, the other players return.

A race to find the penny begins! Players cannot talk or help each other; they just wander the room looking for the penny. When a player finds the penny, he does not tell anyone or make it obvious where it is hidden. Once found, a player sits and writes where he found the penny. Soon, other players start to locate it and also sit to write. The goal is to avoid being the last person to find the penny since that person gets a strike. Once one player is remaining, everyone reveals their papers at the same time to prove they did actually see the penny and wrote the right location. Players that did not write anything or wrote the wrong place get a strike. Another round begins with a new player hiding the penny (everyone should take a turn). Play repeats. Once a player receives three strikes, he is out. Eventually only two people remain—the winners!

PLUS & MINUS

 # OF PLAYERS: 2 or more
PLAYERS: Nicole, Ashley, Hannah, Aubrey
OBJECTS NEEDED: Deck of Cards

OR MORE

Deal the entire deck face down evenly to all players. Players keep their piles face down in front of them—they should not look at their cards. Play begins by having each player turn over the top two cards from her pile and place them side by side. Each player takes the lower numbered card value and subtracts it from the higher numbered card value (suits do not matter). After subtracting, the player with the highest number wins that round and adds all the other player's two cards to her pile.

For example, if Nicole has a 9♣ and a 5♦, she would have 4 (9 - 5 = 4). If 4 is higher than every other player's number, she wins the other players' cards for that hand and adds them to her pile. Players continue to turn over two cards each turn and the person who has the most cards when time is called is the winner! If the game is played with face cards, then the values are as follows:

- Aces = 14 points
- Kings = 13 points
- Queens = 12 points
- Jacks = 11 points

VARIATION: Change things from round to round by alternating subtracting and adding—when adding, the person with largest number wins. Depending on the children's ages, try multiplication as well!

QUARTER TEAM TOSS

 # OF PLAYERS: 2 or more
PLAYERS: Jacob, Ryan, Eric, Justin
OBJECTS NEEDED: Quarters, Bowls

OR MORE

Divide players into teams of two (or play as individuals). Gather three regular dinner bowls (make sure they aren't breakable!), and six quarters for each team (any size coin will work). Mark a throwing line where players stand to throw. About 5' from the line, place the first bowl, then place the second bowl one foot farther, and the last bowl one foot farther than the second. Teams earn points by throwing quarters into the bowls. If a coin lands (and stays) in the closest bowl, it is worth one point. If a player's coin stays in the middle bowl he receives three points, and if a coin stays in the farthest bowl it is worth five points.

Team A starts. Players get three tosses each. After each player on a team has thrown three times, it is the next team's turn. Play continues until one team has reached 50 points and wins the game!

VARIATION: Play using much larger bowls (mixing bowls) and a deck of cards. Each team gets 10 cards per round and tries to toss cards into the three bowls. The respective points for each bowl remain the same.

SEVENS

 # OF PLAYERS: 3 or more
PLAYERS: Alyssa, Aubrey, Nicole, Ashley
OBJECTS NEEDED: Deck of Cards

OR MORE

Deal seven cards to each player and place the remaining cards in a pile in the middle. Flip over the top card from the middle pile to form a discard pile. The player to the left of the dealer, Alyssa, starts by either picking up the top card on the discard pile or the top card (face down) from the center pile. Alyssa chooses a card then discards one card she does not want by placing it on the discard pile. Aubrey is next—she can choose the new top card on the discard pile or one from the center pile. Each turn, players pick up and discard a card, keeping seven cards in hand at all times. Continue until one player has seven cards of the same suit (play with two decks for more players). Once a player does this, she shows her hand to everyone and wins a point. Reshuffle, deal again and start a new round. The first player to score three points is the winner!

VARIATION: For each new round, think of different combinations of seven cards. Examples could include: a run of seven cards (from one to seven in any suit), four of the same cards and then three of the same cards, a run of four and a match of three cards, etc.

SLAP JACK

 # OF PLAYERS: 2 or more
PLAYERS: Andrew, Eric, Justin
OBJECTS NEEDED: Deck of Cards (2 decks for many players)

OR MORE

Deal the deck of cards evenly to all players. The cards are dealt face down, and remain face down throughout the game. The player to the left of the dealer, Andrew, begins by turning over a card from his pile and placing it face up in the middle. Eric does the same, and this continues around the circle. Everyone is anxiously waiting for a Jack to be played. When a Jack is played, the first player to spot it says, "Slap Jack!" and slaps his hand on the middle pile of cards.

Once a Jack has been played and the first person has slapped it, the remaining players quickly place one of their hands on the pile. The last player (or top hand) to hit the pile loses and has to take all the cards in the discard pile and add them to the bottom of his pile of cards. That player then places a new card in the middle, and play continues around the circle. However, if someone mistakenly slaps a card that is not a Jack, that player has to take the whole pile. The goal is to be the first player to get rid of all his cards—that player earns a point. Start another round and deal again. The first player to score three points is the winner!

STRATEGIC BOWLING

 # OF PLAYERS: 2 or more
PLAYERS: Ryan, Justin, Hannah, Ashley
OBJECTS NEEDED: 10 Plastic Cups, Tennis Ball

OR MORE

Set up 10 cups close to each other in bowling pin formation (a triangle with 4 in the back row, 3 in front of those, 2 in front of those, and 1 in front). Cups should be relatively close together—about 4 inches between each cup (close enough that if one cup falls it could hit another cup, but not right next to each other). One cup is designated the *king* cup and the object is NOT to knock over that cup. The placement of the *king* cup will always be in the center (in the middle of the row of 3 cups). Around the cups is a circle about 12' in diameter—each player must stand outside the circle when bowling.

Play begins by having the first person take the tennis ball (or any small ball) and bowl the ball toward the cups. The player must bowl from outside the circle, but anywhere around the circle is fair. Each player gets three rolls per turn. The goal is to knock over as many cups as possible in those three rolls without knocking over the *king* cup. After three bowls, the player receives a point for each cup he knocked over (if the *king* cup is still standing). If any of the three bowls knocks over the *king* cup, that player's turn is over and he receives no points. Players take turns until one player reaches 100 points to win the game!

TOOTHPICK STACK

 # OF PLAYERS: 2 or more
PLAYERS: Alyssa, Eric, Jacob, Nicole
OBJECTS NEEDED: 40-50 Toothpicks, Water Bottle

OR MORE

Place a bottle in the middle of the table. Each player starts with 15 toothpicks. The goal is to be the first player to get rid of all of her toothpicks. Going to the left around the circle, Alyssa takes one of her toothpicks and places it on (across) the top of the bottle (simply lay the toothpick across the opening of the bottle). Eric does the same, laying a toothpick next to or on top of the other toothpick(s). Players do not want to knock off any toothpicks! Each player takes a turn, and play continues around the circle until someone knocks some (or all) of the toothpicks off the bottle. The player who made the toothpicks fall must add them to his pile. The first player to get rid of all his toothpicks receives a point. Start another round—the first person to score three points is the winner!

WAR

 # OF PLAYERS: 2 or more
PLAYERS: Ryan, Eric, Nicole, Ashley
OBJECTS NEEDED: Deck of Cards

OR MORE

The game is played with two players at a time, but games are quick so other players can rotate in. To begin, deal all the cards evenly, face down, between the two players. The players do not look at their cards. At "Go," each player begins turning over the top card from his pile and placing it in the center, face up. The player with the higher card value takes both cards and adds them to his pile (simply place them to the side in a winnings pile). (Keep in mind that an Ace beats a King, a King beats a Queen, etc.)

Occasionally, however, both players will play a similar card (for example, they both play a 5). When that happens, it's WAR! Each player takes one of his cards and places it face down on the middle pile, and then places another card face up on the pile. From the two cards face up, the highest card gets to take all six cards (the two that started the war plus the four that were just played). If there is another tie, the war continues until one person plays a higher card. Play continues until one player has won all the cards (if others are waiting to play, it can be whoever has the most cards after a designated time). If others do rotate in, the winner receives a point and stays to play the next player. The first person to score three points is the winner!

VARIATION: Play this fun game with three people. The game is played the same way, but the person who played the highest card out of the three wins the hand. If the highest card ties with another person, those two players go to War. If all three cards tie each other, then all three are at War (everyone places one card face down and one card face up, until one person wins them all).

WHO, WHERE, WHEN, WHAT, WHY

 # OF PLAYERS: 3 or more
PLAYERS: Alyssa, Hannah, Nicole, Aubrey
OBJECTS NEEDED: Nothing

OR MORE

Aubrey starts this game by thinking of a random object. The goal for the other players is to ask specific questions to try to be the first to discover what the object is. Players take turns guessing going around the circle. Players can only ask questions that start with these five words—*who, where, when, what* or *why*. For example, if Aubrey chose a *book,* Alyssa chooses any of the five types of questions to try to discover what the object is. She may ask, "*Who* would use *it?*" Aubrey answers the question briefly, without telling them what *it* is, but still answering honestly. She could reply, "Everyone." Such an answer is truthful (while vague) and does not give *it* away.

Hannah might ask, "*Where* do you use *it?*" Aubrey responds carefully since a question like this is tricky. If she replies, "Library," it may give the object away—perhaps "school" or "home" might be a better answer. Regardless of her answer, she must always respond truthfully to each question asked (and each answer must be different—no repeating answers). Players continue to take turns asking questions using the five specific words to start the question, and the first person to discover what *it* is receives one point. Players can only make a guess on their own turns and they are limited to three guesses per round. If a player's third guess is not correct, she cannot guess any more during that round. The person who guesses correctly starts another round and chooses a new object. The first to score three points wins!

 # OF PLAYERS: 2 or more

PLAYERS: Andrew, Ryan, Ashley

OBJECTS NEEDED: Nothing

Not Spelling a Word: Play begins by having one person say any letter. Going around the circle to the right, the next person says another letter and the next person another one, etc. The object of the game is to avoid being the person who spells a complete word (words must be longer than three letters). Each time a player says a letter, he must have a real word in mind. For example, if the first three letters are *T, A* and *L,* then the next letter said cannot be an *L* or a *K* because both of those letters would complete a word (and be longer than three letters). If a player does use a letter that completes a word, he gets a strike—and three strikes eliminates a player from the game. However, a player can challenge the person before him if he doesn't think she has a legitimate word in mind (players can only challenge the person who said the last letter). If a player challenges and the last player did not have a legitimate word in mind, the last player gets a strike...but if the player who challenged is wrong, he gets a strike.

Complete Sentence: Much like the *Not Spelling a Word* game, players must not complete a sentence. Play begins by having everyone decide on a letter. If *B* is the letter, then everyone in turn goes around the circle and formulates a sentence using words that start with "B." The sentence has to be longer than three words, and players cannot use more than three adjectives or descriptive words of a noun. If a player does complete a sentence, she gets a strike. An example sentence might be: "Beans bake beautifully behind barricaded, bulging, bent buildings." The sentence is longer than three words, and there are only three adjectives allowed (barricaded, bulging, bent). The person who said *buildings* finished the sentence, so she earned a strike. The person who got the strike chooses a different letter, and starts another round. Three strikes eliminate a player from the game.

Categories: The first person starts by thinking of a random category. Example categories include fruits, cars, sports, vegetables, colors, flowers, animals, etc. If *sports* is the category chosen, the first player starts by naming a sport. The next person must name a different sport, and this continues around the circle. Play continues until someone cannot think of another item in that category, or he says something that has already been said. Players have 10 seconds per turn. If a player does not say a word in time or accidentally repeats one already said, he receives a strike. Three strikes eliminate a player from the game. The last person playing is the winner!

Adjective Letters: One player chooses a letter, and then says a random sentence that has an adjective describing a noun. For example, the letter chosen may be an *A*, and the sentence might be, "My neighbor is an *Angry* man." *Angry* is the adjective and starts with an *A*. Going to the left, the next player must say the same sentence, but use a different adjective that also starts with the same letter. That player might say: "My neighbor is an *Awesome* man." A player only has five seconds to say a sentence, or she gets a strike. Play continues until one player cannot think of a new adjective, or does not say one in time. Once a player gets a strike, she chooses a new letter and says another sentence. Play repeats. Once a player gets three strikes, she is out. The last person left in the game wins!

Backward Spelling: One person chooses any random word (use a dictionary if needed). The player to the left then has to spell that word backwards. There is no time limit. Once a player says a letter, no going back or changing the letter is allowed. For example, if the word is *Riddle,* the next player should say: E L D D I R. That player chooses a word for the next player to spell backward. If a player makes a mistake, he gets a strike. Three strikes eliminate a player from the game.

Speed Syllables: The goal is to say a word with the right amount of syllables, and avoid getting three strikes. The first round everyone says a word with one syllable (example: Hat). The next time around, players must say a word with two syllables (example: Pizza). The next time around the word must have three syllables, then four, etc. A player only has five seconds to answer and cannot say a word that has been previously said. If a player repeats a word or doesn't say one in time, she gets a strike. Three strikes eliminate a player from the game.

Synonym Chain: A synonym is a word that is very similar in definition to another word. For example, synonyms for the word *wonderful* include amazing, awesome, excellent, incredible, outstanding, remarkable, superb, terrific, tremendous, etc. The first player says any word. Going around the circle to the left, each player must say a new synonym for that word. If a player does not respond within five seconds, or says a synonym that has already been said, or does not give a relevant example, he receives a strike. After someone makes a mistake, he chooses another word and play repeats. After a player receives three strikes, he is out. (Try playing this game with antonyms—words that have the opposite meaning as the word chosen.)

CHILDREN'S GAMES
·········· OUTDOORS ··········

ABC'S

 # OF PLAYERS: 2 or more
PLAYERS: Aubrey, Eric, Jacob
OBJECTS NEEDED: Nothing

OR MORE

The goal is to be the first player in the car to find every letter in the alphabet before any other player. For a letter to count, it has to be outside (not in the car). Players can look for letters on anything—signs, billboards, stores, license plates, etc. Players must also go in order from A to Z—they cannot move to a *B* until an *A* is found. The first player to reach *Z* is the winner!

VARIATION: Play as teams. Each team has two players. The first person has to find the *A* and the second person has to find the *B*, etc. (To avoid cheating, players can also be required to call the letter they found and where they found it.)

VARIATION: The letter *must* be the first letter of a word—so for the letter *E,* players cannot use the word *Paper,* they would need to find a word like *Exit*, etc.

BILLBOARD POETRY

 # OF PLAYERS: 2 or more
PLAYERS: Eric, Ryan
OBJECTS NEEDED: Nothing

OR MORE

One player begins by reading a short sentence from a random billboard (anywhere from 5-7 words). Once the sentence is read, the person to the left of whoever just read the sentence has 30 seconds to think up a line that rhymes with the sentence. This made up rhyme must be about the same amount of words, the end word must rhyme and it should be somewhat relating to or relevant to the sentence's meaning. For example, if Eric reads, "Everything in the store must go." Then, before 30 seconds is up, Ryan might say, "The merchandise is selling so slow."

Once Ryan responds with a pertinent rhyme, he will now choose a new sentence and the next player will have to think of a rhyme. Play continues around the circle. If a player does not respond within 30 seconds, or the other players vote that the rhyme is either not rhyming or not related to the sentence read, that player gets one strike. A player is out for that round once he receives three strikes, and the last player remaining once everyone has received three strikes is the winner!

BLIND MAN'S HUNT

 # OF PLAYERS: 4 or more
PLAYERS: Caleb, Hannah, Aubrey, Eric
OBJECTS NEEDED: Blindfold

OR MORE

One person is chosen to be *it*, and is blindfolded. The other players start by standing near *it*. At "Go," *it* spins around five times. As *it* is spinning, everyone else runs in various directions. Once *it* has done five full spins, she yells, "Freeze!" All those running must stop where they are. Then, the goal for *it* is to find and tag the other players—while wearing the blindfold!

As *it* goes to find the other players, there are two ways to locate them: by touch or by hearing. Before each round, everyone decides which one of the two *it* will do. For *touch*: *it* will walk around blindfolded and try to find frozen players—if *it* touches a player, he is out. Players who are frozen must remain where they stopped without moving their feet, but they can duck to avoid *it* when he comes near. For *hearing*: *it* walks around trying to find frozen players, but if *it* comes within 5' of a player, that player must make a noise (and continue making a noise until *it* has left the 5' area). Players, however, try to disguise their voices. Once *it* hears someone, he must guess who is making the noise. If *it* guesses right, that player is out. If *it* guesses wrong, that player is safe and *it* must move on and find someone else (*it* can't come back to that player until he has found and guessed a different player). The last person found receives a point. Start another round with players taking turns being *it*. The first player to score three points is the winner!

CAR HUNT

 # OF PLAYERS: 2 or more
PLAYERS: Alyssa, Eric
OBJECTS NEEDED: Papers, Pencils

OR MORE

Each player writes 20-30 different car types on a piece of paper. Players need to have the same cars written on their lists. The object of the game is to be the first player to find 15 of the listed cars. The first player to do so receives a point, and a new round starts. Each round can have a different objective, and some examples of ways to play rounds include: the first to find three of the same cars receives a point; the first to find five specific cars; the first to find five different makes within the same model (five cars that Ford makes); etc. Be creative—anything goes! The first player to score five points is the winner! Examples of cars include:

Accord, Audi, Blazer, Bronco, BMW, Cadillac, Camry, Chevy, Chrysler, Civic, Corolla, Corvette, Dodge, Escort, Excursion, Expedition, Explorer, Honda, Hummer, Hyundai, Infiniti, Kia, Lexus, Lincoln, Malibu, Mazda, Mercedes, Mustang, Navigator, Odyssey, Pathfinder, Porsches, PT Cruiser, Ram, Ranger, Saturn, Suburban, Tahoe, Taurus, Toyota, Venture, Villager, Volkswagen, Voyager, Windstar, etc.

CATEGORIES CHASE

 # OF PLAYERS: 4 or more
PLAYERS: Jacob, Eric, Nicole, Alyssa
OBJECTS NEEDED: Nothing

Mark a *starting line* and about 20' from it mark a *middle line*. Players need to start behind the *starting line*. One player begins by being *it* and stands 25' from the *starting line* (5' beyond the *middle line*). The player who is *it* faces away from everyone else. *It* chooses a random category and announces it to the other players (examples of categories include animals, flowers, fruits, colors, etc.). All the other players choose something from that category without telling anyone else. For example, if *fruit* is the category, one player might choose *apple,* another might choose *banana,* etc. (it is ok if more than one player chooses the same thing).

It starts by randomly calling various items from the category. When a player's item is called, his goal is to make it down to the *middle line* and back to the *starting line* without *it* tagging him. Keep in mind that *it* is facing the other direction, so players should try to be sneaky and quiet so *it* does not hear them. When *it* hears someone moving, he turns around and tries to tag anyone who has left the *starting line*. If *it* tags someone, that player becomes *it*. As *it* chases players, once they get back across the *starting line* they are safe. But a player cannot leave the *starting line* until her item is called.

To prevent *it* from turning around all the time, *it* can only turn around ten times in a round. After the 10th time, if *it* has not tagged anyone, everyone else receives one point and a new *it* is chosen. Each time a player makes it to the *middle line* and back to the *starting line* without being tagged, she receives a point. For some categories, it may be necessary for *it* to repeat items already said from the category to entice people back out (this way, players could potentially gain more points). The tagged player becomes *it* and a new category is chosen. The first player to reach 20 points is the winner!

VARIATION: This same game can be played in a swimming pool with players swimming quietly to a certain point and back without being tagged.

CIRCLE OF MADNESS

 # OF PLAYERS: 6 or more
PLAYERS: Everyone!
OBJECTS NEEDED: Shoe for Each Player

OR MORE

Gather one shoe for each player and spread them in a large circle. The circle should be roughly 30' in diameter, and each shoe should be at least 10' apart. The shoes signify *safe bases*. One player begins by being *it,* and she stands in the middle of the circle of shoes *(bases)*. The rest of the players each start on a *base*.

The goals for the runners are to run across the circle and stand on another *base* without being tagged by *it,* and to be the last runner tagged. The goal for *it* is to tag everyone twice to end the round. The rules are:

- A runner cannot run to a *base* next to the base she is on.
- There can only be one person on a base at a time.
- Players cannot stand on a base for more than 10 seconds (if they do, it counts as one of their two tags).
- Runners can only run 5' past the *bases*—if they run past the 5' barrier or are tagged at any time, it counts as one tag.

Players continue to run around the *bases* trying not to be tagged by *it*. Once a player is tagged twice, she is out for that round and sits on the sideline. The last player running around receives one point. Start another round—everyone should take a turn being *it*. The first player to score three points is the winner!

CLOTHESPIN GRAB

 # OF PLAYERS: 3 or more
PLAYERS: Jacob, Hannah, Aubrey
OBJECTS NEEDED: Bag of Clothespins

OR MORE

Designate a playing area roughly 30' x 30' large (forming out of bounds lines). Everyone clips three clothespins to their shirts in random places (sleeves, neck, back, etc.). At "Go," players run around and try to grab the clothespins off the other players' shirts and place them on their own shirts. While doing this, they try to prevent others from grabbing their clothespins. Each child is trying to be the one with the most clothespins on her shirt when time is called.

As the children run around and grab clothespins, there is no shoving, pushing or grabbing—children can only run and spin around to avoid losing a clothespin. Children must stay inside the out of bounds lines. When a player takes a clothespin from another player, that person places the new clothespin on his shirt while still running. Players can only take one clothespin at a time. A player cannot take a clothespin from a person she last took one from until she grabs another one from a different opponent. Play continues for about three minutes, then time is called. Players receive one point for every clothespin they are wearing when time is called. Start another round by having everyone start again with three clothespins. The child with the most points after three rounds is the winner!

COPS & ROBBERS

 # OF PLAYERS: 6 or more
PLAYERS: Everyone!
OBJECTS NEEDED: Plastic Cup

OR MORE

Divide players into two equal teams—one team starts by being the *cops* and the other begins as the *robbers*. Designate a 10' circle as the *cops* circle. The *robbers* will have two 10' circles—each about 30 yards away in both directions. Place a plastic cup inside the *cops* circle—this is the item the *robbers* are trying to steal. The goal of the *robbers* is to steal the cup and get it back to one of their circles, while the goal of the *cops* is to place every *robber* in jail. The *cops* also designate a *jail* that is a 10' x 10' square in a random place near the *cops* circle.

To begin, the *cops* stand inside their circle and count to 100 while the *robbers* go and hide. After counting, the *cops* go and try to capture the *robbers* by tagging them, but they also need to protect their cup so it is not stolen. When a *cop* tags a *robber,* the *robber* goes to jail. A *robber* can be released from jail if a teammate tags her while in jail, but only one player can be released at a time. The *cops* are not allowed to closely guard their circle or the jail—only one *cop* can be within 5' of the *cop* circle, and the same rule applies to the *cop* jail. Only one *robber* is allowed in the *cops* circle at one time. If the *robbers* capture the cup and get it back to one of their two circles, they win the round. If the *robber* is tagged on the way back, she goes to the jail and the cup is returned to the *cops* circle. If the *cops* tag and place every *robber* in jail, they win the round. The team that wins the round receives one point. The two teams switch roles and play continues until one team scores five points to win the game!

FOUR SQUARE

 # OF PLAYERS: 4 or more
PLAYERS: Andrew, Eric, Nicole. Aubrey
OBJECTS NEEDED: Round Ball, Sidewalk Chalk

Draw four 6' x 6' squares on a driveway or a street with sidewalk chalk—place two squares on top of the other two squares to form one large square. One square is designated the *king* square. Players are trying to make it to the *king* square. The other three squares are numbered 1, 2 and 3 (#1 is the worst or beginning square).

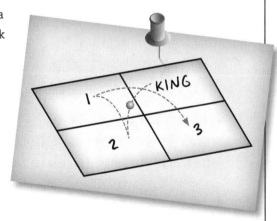

One player stands in each of the 4 squares—if others are playing, they stand to the side and will rotate in. Andrew is standing in the *king* spot. He has the ball and gets to choose any random action that all the other players must do (see examples below). The *king* starts by tossing/bouncing the ball around the circle. Each player must do what the *king* chose. For each action and turn, players must do the action and catch the ball after the first bounce (if necessary). If a player makes a mistake by not doing the right action, or the ball bounces out of bounds, he goes down to the #1 square and everyone else moves up. (If more than four people are playing, the person who made a mistake goes to the end of the line and the next person rotates in at the #1 square.) Play continues as players try to work up to the *king* spot.

Explanations of various actions a *King* can choose:
- *Around the World*—the ball is bounced from square to square in a circular pattern.
- *Categories*—the King chooses a category, and as everyone bounces the ball, players have to name something from that category before they pass the ball. Players only have three seconds to do so, and they can't say something that's already been said.
- *One Handed*—players can only hit the ball back and forth between squares with one hand.
- *Skyscrapers*—players have to bounce the ball in an opponent's square as high as they can, then the player whose square it bounced in has to catch the ball before it hits the ground (if she doesn't, she is out).
- *Mini's*—players bounce the ball as low as they can in any square.
- *Cherry Bomb*—players bounce the ball as hard as they can at a player (he has to catch it before it falls).
- *Clap Throw*—the first person throws the ball into the air and claps three times before the ball touches the ground, and then catches it after it bounces. The next player has to clap four times, the next player five times, etc.
- *Spinners*—players have to spin after they pass the ball.
- *Battle*—two players only pass the ball back and forth.
- *Etc.*—make up anything!

FREEZE B-A-L-L

 # OF PLAYERS: 3 or more
PLAYERS: Ryan, Ashley, Jacob, Nicole
OBJECTS NEEDED: Ball, Sidewalk Chalk

....

Each player chooses a number from 1-10, but no player can have the same number. Players need to remember both their own number and the other players' numbers. Using sidewalk chalk, draw an 8' circle on the sidewalk, street, etc. Everyone starts by standing inside the circle. One player takes the ball and throws it into the air (the higher the better). While the ball is in the air, the player who threw it yells another player's number. The player whose number was called must try to catch or get the ball quickly (it's okay if the ball bounces, but the sooner it is caught, the better). While the ball is in the air, all the other players run quickly away from the circle in various directions. Once the person catches the ball (she must be holding it and standing inside the circle), she yells, "Freeze!" At "Freeze!" everyone must stop immediately.

The person who caught the ball then tries to hit another player by rolling (or bouncing) the ball from within the circle. The other players must keep both feet on the ground and cannot move or dodge the ball. If a player is hit by the ball, he gets a '*B.*' Everyone comes back to the circle, and the person who just caught the ball now throws it in the air and calls another number. Play repeats— as players continue to get hit with the ball, they spell B.A.L.L. Once a player has been hit four times (spelled B.A.L.L.) he is out for that round and must stand to the side. The last player remaining receives a point. The person to score three points first is the winner!

HOPPING ELIMINATION

 # OF PLAYERS: 2 or more
PLAYERS: Alyssa, Ryan
OBJECTS NEEDED: Sidewalk Chalk

....

Draw two circles on the driveway or the street using sidewalk chalk. The first

circle should be just large enough for someone to stand in (about 2' x 2' wide). The second circle should surround the smaller circle—it should be roughly 4' x 4' wide. Write *Home* inside the inner circle and draw lines on the outer circle to divide it into 10 equal sections. Number the sections in the outer circle from 1 - 10. (To make even circles, tie a string around the piece of chalk and hold the loose end at the center of the circle while moving the chalk.)

The goal is to hop through each section from 1 - 10, then hop into the *Home* circle. Hopping can be done on one foot, both feet, or alternating between feet. If a player touches a line when hopping, or hops outside the borders of the larger circle, he loses his turn. If a player makes it safely all the way through sections 1 - 10 and hops into the *Home* circle, she gets to take the chalk and write her name inside any of the 10 hopping sections.

After a name(s) is written in a section, no other player can hop in that section—only the person whose name is written inside is allowed to hop there. If another player also makes it all the way around and into *Home*, he, too, writes his name in any section. As the round progresses, sections continue to be claimed. When it becomes impossible for players to hop to *Home*, or all the sections have been filled, the player whose name appears the most in the squares receives a point. Erase the names to start another round. The first player to score five points is the winner!

JAIL DODGEBALL

 # OF PLAYERS: 6 or more
PLAYERS: Everyone!
OBJECTS NEEDED: Many Balls

OR MORE

Gather enough balls so that there is one for each person playing—the balls should be softer balls so that nobody gets hurt. Designate a playing area roughly 20 x 20 yards, either outside or in a gym. Ensure that everyone knows where the boundary lines are, and divide the area in half to create a *middle line*. Divide players into two equal teams and have each team stand on one side of the *middle line*. Each team's goal is to throw the balls back and forth to try and hit every player on the opposing team.

Each team starts with half of the balls. When a player is hit, she must go to the *jail* of the other team. The *jail* for each team is simply behind the far end boundary line on both sides. Players cannot leave the boundaries at any time during the game or they are out and must go to their opponent's *jail*. Players can only be released from *jail* if a ball rolls out of bounds. The first person in jail to retrieve an out of bounds ball gets to throw it at one of the players on the opposing team. She can throw it from any spot out of bounds and if she does hit an opponent, that opponent goes to *jail* and the person who was in *jail* gets to go back to her team's side and start throwing again.

To avoid injuries, a ball cannot be thrown at someone's head (if this happens, the person who threw it goes to *jail*). If someone catches a ball thrown at him, the person who threw it must go to *jail*. Each team tries to hit opponents with balls and tries to catch balls thrown at them. Teams also try to prevent balls from rolling out of bounds because a player in *jail* from the opposing team could throw it back in and hit one of their teammates. Play continues until one team sends every player from the opposing team to *jail* to win the game!

LICENSE PLATE FUN (7 GAMES)

 # OF PLAYERS: 2 or more
PLAYERS: Hannah, Ryan, Jacob
OBJECTS NEEDED: Nothing

OR MORE

For that next long road trip, or just a short trip to run errands, kids can play these fun games with license plates:

License Plate ABCs: Be the first player to find every letter in the alphabet, going in order from A-Z (or backward from Z-A), using license plates.

Doubles & Triples: Find any two letters, or any two numbers, that are the same, on one license plate. The numbers/letters do not have to be right by each other, just somewhere on the license plate. Then, do the same with triple letters and numbers. Doubles earn two points and triples are worth three points. The first player to 20 points wins!

50 States Search: Each player needs a list of the U.S. states. When a player finds a license plate from a state, he crosses it off the list. The first player to find 20 states is the winner! An alternative is to list the states that are close to where you live or near states you'll be driving through, and the first player to find three license plates from each state on the list is the winner!

Palindromes: A palindrome is a word (or set of numbers) that is the same backward. Examples: 525, 6996, 22 ... or *did, civic, gig, kayak,* etc. The first player to find three palindromes wins!

Phrase Competition: Players take turns creating phrases from the letters on a passing car's license plate (if there are only numbers on the plate, wait for another car). The number of letters on the license plate doesn't matter, the game is on! For example, if the license plate has PAR 198—the player thinks of a phrase for P A R. Perhaps she might say, "Pandas are rare!" The rule is that the phrase must make sense (a logical phrase or structure of words). The phrase does not have to be a complete sentence, but the word combinations have to be related and make sense. Players earn a strike if they fail to say a proper phrase (the other players can judge), or they do not say something within 10 seconds (or before the next car passes in that lane). Three strikes eliminate a player from the game. The last player wins!

Speedy Words: Players look out the passenger side of the car. When a car passes, they look at that car's license plate and race to be the first player to shout a (correct) word that has all the letters from the plate. For example, if the license plate was PCG 468, someone might shout, "Packing!" The player that shouts the first correct word receives a point. Wait for another car and repeat—the first person to five points wins!

License Plate Bingo: Draw 25 boxes on a piece of paper (5 rows x 5 columns). In each box, write a certain thing that the players must find. Make the things hard or simple depending upon the age group playing. Examples include a license plate with the numbers 1, 2 and 3, the letters *R* and *S* by each other, a license plate from Colorado, three license plates from one state other than your own, a real word on a plate, one with only letters or numbers, etc. Play various rounds by trying to get five in a row, an X shape, a black out, etc.

MAD RUSH

 # OF PLAYERS: 6 or more
PLAYERS: Everyone!
OBJECTS NEEDED: Nothing

OR MORE

Designate a *home base* circle that is about 10' in diameter. Around the circle draw another circle that is roughly 15' in diameter. Divide players into two equal teams. Team A starts by standing in *home base*, closing their eyes and counting to 100. While Team A counts, Team B separates and hides in random places.

Once Team A has counted, their goal is to find and tag everyone on Team B, while protecting their *home base*. Team B's goal is to get as many players as possible back to *home base* without being tagged by Team A. Players from Team B can stay hidden until found, or make mad dashes to *home base*—they simply do not want to be tagged by someone on Team A. If a player is tagged, he is out and must sit on the sidelines until the next round. When a player makes it to *home base* without being tagged by someone on Team A, his team receives one point (that player will wait in *home base* until the round is done). Team A's players cannot enter the larger circle at any time. The round ends when everyone has either been tagged or made it back to *home base* safely. Teams switch places and play repeats. The first team to score 30 points wins!

MEMORIES

 # OF PLAYERS: 2 or more
PLAYERS: Hannah, Jacob, Aubrey
OBJECTS NEEDED: Nothing

Think of a random memory from the past that all the players shared. It can be anything—a previous road trip, visiting the grandparents, a trip to a theme park, a favorite summer vacation, a special Christmas, a certain birthday, a sporting event, etc. One person starts by telling everyone one thing she remembers about that experience/memory. Going in a circle to the left, the next person says something different he remembers about the same experience. This repeats around the circle, but don't make a mistake! If a player doesn't answer within 10 seconds, says something that has already been said, or says something that did not actually happen during that experience, he gets a strike (the other players judge). The player who gets a strike thinks of a new memory, and play continues. Once a person gets three strikes, he is out. The last person playing is the winner!

MILES OF NUMBERS

 # OF PLAYERS: 2 or more
PLAYERS: Andrew, Aubrey, Justin, Eric
OBJECTS NEEDED: Nothing

This exciting game is more than just counting—it can be mentally frustrating, somewhat challenging and a lot of fun! The goal is for everyone to count to 100, but with a few special twists. Play begins by having the first player say, "One." The next player says, "Two," and the next player says, "Three," all the way up to 100. Each player takes a turn saying a number, and play goes around the circle to the left.

When a player comes to any number that has a 6 in it or is a divisible by 6, she must say "*beep*" in the place of that number. For example, if a player comes to any of these numbers she says *beep*: 6, 12, 16, 18, 24, 26, 30, 36, etc. If a player makes a mistake and does not say *beep* when she should, she gets a strike. Play resumes from the number that the previous person missed. Once 100 is reached, the games starts over. Each round the players decide whether to keep 6 as the *beep* number, or choose another number and play the same way. Play continues until players get three strikes and are out. The last player still in the game is the winner!

MINIATURE BASEBALL

 # OF PLAYERS: 2 or more
PLAYERS: Nicole, Justin, Ryan, Ashley
OBJECTS NEEDED: Sidewalk Chalk, 2 Rocks (or coins)

OR MORE

Draw a baseball diamond on the driveway or street with sidewalk chalk. Draw the foul ball lines—two lines about 10' long, going in perpendicular directions (forming a V shape). Draw first base about half way down the right side foul line (about 5' away). First base is simply a circle about 2' in diameter placed about 2' from the foul ball line. Draw 2nd base about 3'-4' from 1st base and about 5' from home base. The 2nd base circle should be a little smaller,

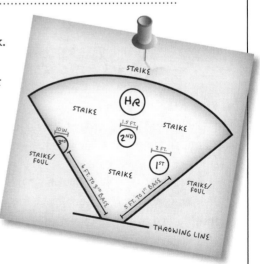

roughly about 1.5' in diameter. Draw 3rd base about half way down the left foul ball line (about 6' away), making this circle even smaller—about 10" in diameter and very close to the left foul ball line. Home base is simply the corner where the two lines meet. Roughly 10' away from home base in center field is a 2' circle—this is the *Home Run* (HR) circle.

The goal is to play baseball by tossing a rock (or coin) and trying to make it land inside one of the circles. Nicole begins by standing behind home base and tossing the rock (neither her body nor her arm can extend past home base). She may want to play it safe and aim for 1st base, or go for it all and try for a HR. If the rock lands in a circle, then it is a hit, and a *ghost runner* is on that base. Nicole picks up her rock and tosses again—she keeps tossing until she gets three outs. For example, if her first throw landed in the circle for 2nd base, and her next throw landed in the 3rd base circle, then she has a ghost runner on 3rd and she scores a point because the ghost runner from 2nd base got back to home base when she made her second hit.

When a player tosses the rock and it lands anywhere outside a circle or outside the foul ball lines, it counts as a strike. Like baseball—three strikes make an out and three outs change the inning. After the third out, the next player takes his turn tossing. Play repeats, and the player with the most points after five innings is the winner!

MINI BOCCE

 # OF PLAYERS: 2 or more
PLAYERS: Alyssa, Eric, Jacob, Aubrey
OBJECTS NEEDED: Paper Plate for Each Player, Pair of Socks

OR MORE

Each player writes his name on a paper plate. To begin, one player takes a pair of socks and throws it in front of everyone about 10'-15' away. Players take turns throwing their paper plates (like Frisbees®) toward the pair of socks. The goal is to have the plate closest to the pair of socks. After each player throws, the player whose plate is on or closest to the socks receives a point. That player then tosses the pair of socks as far away and in any direction as he chooses. Another round starts and players again toss their plates toward the socks. Play continues like this, and the first player to score 10 points is the winner!

MODIFIED HORSESHOES

 # OF PLAYERS: 2 or more
PLAYERS: Aubrey, Jacob
OBJECTS NEEDED: Blanket, Bucket, 3 Tennis Balls

OR MORE

Let's be honest—how many people actually have real horseshoes? This version of the classic game is adapted for everyone. Place a small blanket flat on the ground with a bucket in the middle. Players stand about 20' from the bucket and take turns trying to get the balls to land in the bucket. Players toss three tennis balls per turn. Players rotate turns. After everyone has had five turns, the player with the most points wins the game!

SCORING

- If a player throws a ball and it hits the blanket, but rolls or bounces off, it is worth one point.
- If the ball stays on the blanket, it is worth two points.
- If the ball hits the bucket, but rolls or bounces off, it is worth two points.
- If the ball hits the bucket and stays on the blanket, it is worth three points.
- If the ball lands and stays inside the bucket, it is worth 10 points.
- If the ball knocks the bucket over, simply score as above and reset the bucket.

NUMBERS WALL BALL

 # OF PLAYERS: 4 or more
PLAYERS: Hannah, Eric, Ryan, Justin
OBJECTS NEEDED: Tennis Ball

This fun game is played against a wall that doesn't have any windows—the side of the house, garage door, fence, building, etc. Players should be numbered (if there are four players, number them 1, 2, 3 and 4). All the players line up 10' from the wall, side by side, facing it. Players bounce balls off the wall trying to get the next player in line out. Players can throw the ball as hard or as softly as they want, and in any direction.

One player starts by throwing the ball against the ground to bounce it off the wall (balls must bounce on the ground first, then bounce up and off the wall for the throw to count). When the first person throws the ball, she calls another player's number (she should call the number as she releases the ball). For example, if she calls the number 2, the player whose number is 2 (Eric) must catch the ball before it bounces twice (after it hits the wall). After Eric catches the ball, he must stand where he caught the ball and take his turn throwing it against the wall. He, too, calls a player's number.

If a player does not catch the ball by the second bounce, he receives a strike. A player also receives a strike if he makes a bad throw, the ball hits the wall first, or it bounces twice before hitting the wall. Once a player receives three strikes, he is out for that round. Play continues until one player gets everyone else out. That player receives a point for winning the round. The first person to win three rounds is the winner!

OCTOPUS

 # OF PLAYERS: 4 or more
PLAYERS: Ryan, Justin, Ashley, Nicole
OBJECTS NEEDED: Nothing

OR MORE

Establish a *starting line* and a *middle line* about 30' apart. These parallel lines should be roughly 40' long. Designate side boundaries so the playing area forms a large square. Draw or mark a small 2' wide circle in the middle of the play area.

The game begins with Ryan being *it.* He starts by standing in the middle circle while the remaining players line up along the *starting line.* At "Go," each player tries to run to the *middle line* and back to the *starting line* without being tagged by *it.* If a player does make it from the *starting line* to the *middle line* and back, she receives one point. Players can run anywhere they want, as long as they stay in bounds. If a player runs out of bounds, they are considered tagged and must go stand anywhere in the playing area. Players continue to run around trying to score points until everyone has been tagged.

It can run around anywhere in the playing area trying to tag others to prevent them from scoring points. Once a player has been tagged, she must stop where she was tagged and remain at that spot for the remainder of the round. Once tagged, these players begin helping *it* by reaching with their arms to try to tag other players as they run past (they have an incentive to do so to prevent others from scoring points). Eventually only one player remains—that person wins that round and receives an extra three points (on top of any other points she got for going between the two lines). Players take turns being *it,* and once everyone has been *it,* the person with the most points wins the game!

RED-ROVER RED-ROVER

OR MORE

 # OF PLAYERS: 6 or more
PLAYERS: Everyone!
OBJECTS NEEDED: Nothing

The kids playing this classic game need to be careful so that nobody gets hurt...but it is a classic for a reason! Divide players into two teams. Teams stand parallel about 20' - 30' apart, facing each other. Each team lines up side by side and holds hands to make a human chain of players. While holding hands, players spread roughly 2' - 3' apart.

The game begins by having Team A decide on a person from Team B that they want to call. Once decided, everyone from Team A collectively says, "Red-Rover Red-Rover, send _____ right over." The team fills in the blank with the name of someone from Team B. For example, if Eric was called, then Eric runs over and tries to break through the arms of any two players on Team A. Breaking through simply means that the two players holding hands let go when Eric runs into their arms. The goal is for these two players to hold on and not let someone break through their team's chain of players. If Eric breaks through, then Eric gets to pick any player from Team A to join his team. Play continues with Team B calling someone from Team A over to their side. If a player does not break through (the two players keep holding hands and do not allow the person to break through), then that player stays on the team that just captured him. Play continues back and forth until one side has captured everybody!

VARIATION: If a player is called over and she does not break through, she goes to the *jail* of that team. The *jail* is simply an area to the side where the captured players stand. Each team needs its own *jail*. Then, when a player is called over and does break through, she gets to take a teammate out of *jail* to rejoin the team (only one player can be released from *jail* at a time). If nobody is in *jail,* then teams simply try to break through so they are not sent to *jail,* and if this happens, they just go back to their own team's side. Play goes back and forth until one team has captured every player.

ROAD TRIP BINGO RACE

 # OF PLAYERS: 2 or more
PLAYERS: Andrew, Hannah
OBJECTS NEEDED: Papers, Pencils

OR MORE

Before your next trip, make a list of various things that you anticipate seeing on the trip. Examples include a boat, an airplane, a river, a lake, a mountain, a camper, a pine tree, a bike, a certain type of car, a bus stop, a restaurant, an animal, a specific city, etc. To make it even more difficult, be more specific—a white car, a red shirt, a bird flying, a motorcycle with two people on it, a cow eating, an airplane at an airport, etc. Simply list 25 random, fun things!

On a different sheet of paper draw 25 boxes—5 rows x 5 columns—to create a Bingo card. Write each of the 25 things in one of the boxes and give a copy to each player. The player who wins each round receives a point, and the person with the most points by the end of the trip is the winner! Try these different ways to play:

- The first player to find five in a row receives a point.
- The first player to find the items on the Bingo card that form an X receives a point.
- The first player to find all the items around the border of the Bingo card receives a point.
- The first player to black out (find all 25 items) receives a point.

ROMAN BALL

 # OF PLAYERS: 4 or more
PLAYERS: Andrew, Aubrey, Nicole, Justin, Eric
OBJECTS NEEDED: Sidewalk Chalk, Bouncy Ball

OR MORE

Draw a 5' circle on the driveway or in the street—this is the *inner circle*. Draw a 20' circle around the *inner circle* to create the *outer circle*. Only four people play this game at a time (if more are playing, they simply rotate in as others receive strikes). All four players stand around the *outer circle* and one player starts with the ball. The object is to throw the ball and have it bounce inside the *inner circle* and land outside the *outer circle,* while trying to throw it so that the other players do not catch it before it bounces again.

After a ball bounces in the *inner circle*, if someone does catch the ball then the player who threw it gets a strike. Those catching must catch it before it bounces outside the *outer circle,* and they cannot go past (inside) the *outer circle* to catch it. If a player throws the ball and it does not first bounce inside the *inner circle,* or it lands before going outside the *outer circle,* that also is a strike for the thrower. Thus, players can throw hard or softly, and bounce it as high or as low as they want as long as it first bounces in the *inner circle* and goes past the *outer circle* before bouncing again. Once a player receives three strikes, he is out for that round. If the ball is bounced across without any player catching it, it earns a point for the player who threw it. Players take turns throwing the ball. If more than four are playing, after a player receives a strike, a new player will rotate in. If a player eliminates everyone from the game, he receives five points (in addition to any points he earned from throwing). Start another round. The first player to score 15 points wins!

SIDEWALK BALL CHALLENGE

 # OF PLAYERS: 2 or more
PLAYERS: Aubrey, Ryan, Jacob
OBJECTS NEEDED: Tennis Ball

OR MORE

The game is played using three consecutive sidewalk squares or sections (or draw three 3' x 3' squares using sidewalk chalk on a driveway or in the street). Number the boxes: Box 1, Strike, Box 2. Player 1 (Aubrey) stands behind her box (Box 1), and Player 2 (Ryan) stands behind his (Box 2), with one sidewalk section between them (the Strike box). Aubrey begins by bouncing the ball so that it passes over the middle square and bounces in Ryan's box. After the ball bounces, Ryan tries to catch the ball before it hits the ground. Then, Ryan throws the ball back, also passing it over the middle section while trying to bounce the ball in Aubrey's box. This repeats back and forth, with players trying to score points according to the rules below. The first player to score 25 points is the winner. If others are playing, once a player gets three outs, he goes to the end of the line and the next person rotates in to play.

RULES

- When the ball bounces in the middle section, the player who threw it gets a strike.
- Three strikes equal an out.
- If a player's throw bounces anywhere outside the other player's box, it is a strike for the player who threw it.
- If the other player catches the ball after the first bounce, it is a strike for the person who threw it.
- To avoid getting strikes, both players should bounce the ball properly and try to get the other player to either drop or miss the pass.
- If a player successfully bounces the ball and the other player does not catch it before it bounces again, the thrower earns a point.

SPACE STATIONS

 # OF PLAYERS: 4 or more
PLAYERS: Nicole, Ryan, Ashley, Jacob
OBJECTS NEEDED: Shoe for Each Player

OR MORE

All but one player places a shoe randomly in a park or open field. Each shoe must be at least 15' apart, but can be placed anywhere. There should be one less shoe than the number of players. One player starts as *it*—in our game it is Nicole. When Nicole yells, "Go," the remaining players run around the playing area for a little while. Whenever *it* wants to, she yells, "Stop!" When "Stop!" is yelled, players must hurry and place a foot on a shoe. A player is safe if he is standing on a shoe, but only one person is allowed on each shoe. Each time, one player is left without a shoe—that player receives a strike and becomes the new *it*.

RULES

- While players are running, they cannot stay by or run around a shoe for more than three seconds.
- Players cannot go back to the same shoe they were just on.
- When hurrying to get to a shoe, a player cannot kick or move a shoe.
- Once a player gets two strikes, he is out for that round and must sit on the sideline until the next round.
- When a player is out, remove one shoe and resume play.
- The last two people playing in a round each receive one point.
- The first player to score three points is the winner!

TAG VARIATIONS (6 TOTAL)

 # OF PLAYERS: 2 or more
PLAYERS: Andrew, Ryan, Hannah, Alyssa
OBJECTS NEEDED: Nothing

OR MORE

The classic game of tag will always be a favorite but try these variations for some spice and diversity!

Triangle Tag: Divide players into teams of four. Each team starts with three players holding hands to form a triangle around the 4th teammate standing in the middle. The player in the middle is both the *tagger,* and the person trying to be tagged by the other teams. Everyone is *it* in this fun game! At "Go," each team moves around together in this formation trying to tag another team by simply touching the middle player. Once the player in the middle has been tagged, that player switches places with a teammate so a new player is in the middle and play continues.

RULES

- The three teammates forming a triangle can never let go of each other. If this happens, it counts as a tag.

- The middle player can reach outside of the triangle while tagging and duck to avoid being tagged, but she can never leave the triangle.
- Once each person on the team has been tagged and taken a turn in the middle, that team is out and must sit on the sidelines until the next round.
- The last team in the game is the winner!

Expansion Tag: Designate a 20 x 20 yard area that players must stay within. One player starts as *it* by running around trying to tag the other players. Once he tags the first player, that player joins *it*. *It* and the new person now interlock arms at the elbow and run around together. (The first *it* remains on one end and the new people keep joining the growing end.) When they tag another person, the new player joins the expanding *it*. As *it* gets larger, only the two end people can tag other players (all the middle people just run). The last person tagged receives a point. Start another round with a new *it*. The first player to score three points wins!

Paper, Rock, Scissors Tag: Divide players into two equal teams. Set up two parallel *safe lines* for each team about 30' apart. In the middle of the *safe lines* mark a *middle line*. Each team starts by going to its own side and huddling to decide on *Paper, Rock* or *Scissors*. (Like the classic game of *Paper, Rock, Scissors*, Paper beats Rock, Rock beats Scissors, and Scissors beats Paper).

Both teams come to the *middle line*. The players on each team line up side by side. Teams should be directly across from each other about 3' apart. All at once, everyone says, "Paper, Rock, Scissors, Shoot!" On "Shoot!" each team reveals their team's choice. If there is a tie, simply re-huddle and decide again. The team that wins on "Shoot!" chases the other team to try and tag as many of their players as possible before they have a chance to return to their *safe line*. For example, if Team A chose *Paper* and Team B chose *Rock*—then Team A chases Team B trying to tag as many of them as possible. Players that get tagged are out and must sit on the sidelines until the next round. If a player makes it back to his team's *safe line* before being tagged, he is safe and remains in the game. The team that eliminates its opponents first receives a point. Start a new round with everyone playing again. The first team to score five points wins!

Freeze Tag: Divide players into teams of 2-3 players. One team is *it* first—their goal is to tag everyone in less than five minutes. When a player is tagged, that player must freeze—she must remain in that spot and not move until a teammate tags her to un-freeze her. Once an entire team has been frozen, they are out for that round. Each round is only five minutes long—at the end of five minutes, the team that is *it* gets a point for each team they froze. If a team has even one person who is un-frozen when time is called, that team receives a point. Start another round with a new team as *it*. The first team to 10 points wins!

Jungle Gym Tag: This fun version of tag is played at a park or large jungle gym. Simply play tag, but on a jungle gym. The only rule is that the ground is off-limits. If a player falls or touches the ground, she becomes *it*—and the person who is *it* also cannot touch the ground. There are no tag-backs for at least five seconds.

Flashlight Tag: Each player needs a flashlight since this game is best played in the dark (indoors or outdoors). Flashlights must stay on the entire round. Players cannot shine their lights upward, hold them against their bodies to be unseen, or cover them in any way. One player starts as *it*. This player chases the other players and tries to shine her light on the light of the other players. If she succeeds by shining her light on another's, that person becomes *it*. Lights can't just cross—the actual end of the light (circle portion seen at the end of the light—on the wall or ground) must be tagged by the end of the person's light who is *it*.

Flashlight Tag Variation: The one person who is *it* remains *it* the entire round, and everyone takes turns being *it*. Once a player's light is tagged by the light of *it* (simply touched or lights cross), that person is out, turns off his light and sits on the sidelines until the next round. The last person playing receives a point, and the first player to three points wins!

ULTIMATE RELAY

OR MORE

 # OF PLAYERS: 4 or more
PLAYERS: Andrew, Ryan, Aubrey, Eric
OBJECTS NEEDED: Nothing

Begin by dividing everyone into two teams. Players collectively decide the course together—there should be roughly 10 relay legs for each team to complete. Absolutely anything can be done—be creative!

Sample relay legs:
- Run around the house.
- Ride a bike to the end of the street and back.
- Crab walk across the yard and back, circling a chair in the middle.
- Make a shot in the basketball hoop from the 3-point line.
- Do 20 jumping jacks while racing around chairs.
- Run backwards to touch a neighbor's fence and come back.

At "Go," the first player from each team completes the first leg of the relay. Once done, he tags the next teammate, who must complete the next leg of the relay. This continues until one team completes the relay to win!

VACATION VERBAL CHAIN

OR MORE

 # OF PLAYERS: 2 or more
PLAYERS: Nicole, Aubrey, Hannah, Ashley
OBJECTS NEEDED: Nothing

How good is your memory? In this fun memory game, one player starts by saying, "I am going on a vacation, and I am going to take a _____." The player can fill in the blank with whatever she wants (a suitcase, clothes, money, camera, etc.). Going in a circle to the left, the next player says the same sentence, but repeats the item just said and the person's name—and then adds what she is taking, too. If Nicole was taking some *money* and Aubrey was taking a *camera,* Hannah would say: "I am going on vacation, and Nicole is going to take some *money* and Aubrey is going to take a *camera* and I am going to take a *sweater*." This continues around the circle. If a player does not say the names or items in the proper order, or if she forgets a name or item, she gets a strike. The person who made the mistake starts a new round, and this repeats until everyone has received three strikes and there is only one player left. That player is the winner!

WIDE LEGGED ROLL

 # OF PLAYERS: 4 or more
PLAYERS: Justin, Eric, Jacob, Andrew
OBJECTS NEEDED: Ball

OR MORE

Begin by establishing two team lines about 30' long and 30' apart. Divide players into two teams. Each team stands on its team line across from the other team. Teammates should spread out, side by side, with about 3' between players. Every player stands with feet apart, leaving room between players on a team.

Team A begins with one player taking a ball and rolling it toward the opposing team—the goal is to roll the ball between the legs of another player. Whether the ball goes through the legs of someone or not, Team B takes the ball and rolls it back trying to roll it between the legs of someone from the opposing team. Everyone on each team takes a turn rolling as the ball goes back and forth between teams. If the ball does go through the legs of a player, that player is out for that round and must go sit on the sidelines until the next round starts. Play continues back and forth, and the first team to get everyone out on the opposing team receives a point. Start another round with everyone returning to play. The team that scores five points first wins!

5 COIN TOSS

 # OF PLAYERS: 2 or more

PLAYERS: Andrew, Ryan, Jacob

OBJECTS NEEDED: 5 Coins for Each Player, Sidewalk Chalk

OR MORE

Draw a small circle about 2' in diameter on the sidewalk or street with sidewalk chalk. Enclose the small circle in a larger circle, roughly 4' in diameter. About 8' from the edge of the larger circle, draw a line where the players stand. Each player needs five coins. (Play the game indoors by using yarn or string to designate the circles.)

Taking turns, each player stands at the throwing line and makes five tosses. The goal is to land coins inside the smallest circle. If a coin lands and stays in the inner circle, it is worth three points (the coin can bounce or roll to get there, as long as it stays). If a coin lands outside the small circle, but within the large circle, the toss earns one point. Coins touching any line earn the points of the smallest circle the coin is touching. If the coin lands and stays outside both circles, that coin is out. Once a coin is out, it cannot be used for the rest of that round. Players continue taking turns, but as the game progresses, some players may only have a few coins to toss on their turns since some of their other coins may be out for that round. (Some players may still have five tosses each turn, while others may only have two.) The first player to score 50 points is the winner!

INDEX

CHILDREN'S GAMES

INDOOR & QUIET GAMES

OUTDOOR & ACTIVE GAMES

ROAD TRIP & CAR GAMES

SIDEWALK GAMES

WORDS & NUMBERS GAMES